0059965

D1073862

The Art of Soccer

A Better Way to Play

Mark G. Catlin, M.D.

Illustrations by Carolyn Emory

Photographs by Kingsley LaBrosse, Phil Stephens and Mark Catlin

Soccer Books, St. Paul, MN USA

Published by:

Soccer Books
P.O. Box 4756 - 01
St. Paul, MN 55104

Printed in The United States of America

Cataloging in Publication Data

Catlin, Mark G., 1952 –
Art of Soccer: A Better Way to Play
Includes Index.
1. Soccer (Soccer Football)

GV943.C289   797.C289

ISBN 0–9626834–6–9

Table of Contents

Photo by Phil Stephens

Chapter 1

Space: The Central Concept

"You can be sure of succeeding in your attacks if you only attack places that are undefended." Sun Tzu (The Art of War)

Summary: To win a soccer match one team must score more goals than their opponent. The tasks are to score and prevent the opponent from scoring. The modern tactical approach to these tasks involves space and time. The spaces are areas free of opponents. When a player has the ball in a space they will have time until an opponent arrives. This time without pressure can be used to control the ball, advance, shoot, or wait for others to get open. The ability to influence the distribution of space creates new offensive tactics. Attacking players not only influence space by their position, but also by their movement with the ball, movement without the ball, passing, and beating defenders. Players must learn to be conscious of the constantly changing distribution of space and how they can affect it. On offense, a team creates and uses space; on defense, space is removed by covering individuals or selected areas of the field.

The Game — A Tactical Definition

Although soccer is the world's most popular sport, few of its millions of fans and players find it easy to understand. However, the thousands of individual decisions that create this seemingly complex game are simply based on considerations of space and time. Space is required for the offensive tasks of keeping possession of the ball and scoring goals. Restricting space helps the defense regain possession and prevent goals. The attacking team creates and uses space, the defense attempts to eliminate useful spaces.

Normally, the offense's highest priority is scoring goals, while the defense's principle objective is to prevent goals (Table 1). The relative priority of these tasks varies with the score, the time remaining, and the area of the field. For example, the attacking team takes few risks (because a turnover could result in a goal) and places a high priority on possession when handling the ball in the

Offensive Tasks
1) Score goals
2) Keep possession of the ball

Defensive Tasks
1) Prevent goals
2) Get possession of the ball

Table 1.

2

Figure 1 Going Over

The theoretical basis of many offensive tactics, and in the space theory itself, is avoiding opponents. Since we can't get rid of opponents, the next best thing is to avoid them or limit our contact with them. We avoid them by using areas of the field where they aren't (spaces) and by going over them. Long air-balls successfully bypass many opponents. This scoring attempt came from a corner kick that easily bypassed many defenders because it was in the air.

defensive end of the field. Conversely, in the attacking end risks are taken and possession often jeopardized in an attempt to score. The same considerations apply to defense. In the offensive end risks are taken to regain possession while near the goal being defended the emphasis is on conservative play to prevent goals.

When a team is behind the normal priority of the offensive and defensive tasks may be reversed. However, this alteration is often detrimental. For example, when the defense places a strong emphasis on regaining possession risks are taken in attempting to win the ball and goals may easily be conceded.

While the offensive and defensive tasks are opposites they are inseparable. The offensive task of keeping possession also has an important defensive function — keeping possession is the best way to keep an opponent from scoring. Every minute the team has the ball is one less minute the opponent can use to score. Likewise, defensive roles sometimes serve offensive purposes. This blurring of offensive and defensive tasks makes them intertwined and mutually dependent.

The principal offensive tactical problem is to make possession and offense possible by minimizing the effects of having opponents on the field. There are three basic ways to minimize the disruptive effects of opponents: 1) improve skills, 2) use long passes to bypass most opponents and 3) use areas of the field without opponents (spaces).

Improving fundamental skills may be the most important of these minimizing methods, particularly at the amateur level. A team with a high skill level is less likely to lose the ball by poor trapping, dribbling or passing. Developing skills often benefits a team more than devising sophisticated tactics.

Many defenders can be avoided by using long passes (Fig. 1, pg. 3). The most common examples are corner kicks, goal kicks, goalie punts and long centering passes. In these situations, most opponents are simply avoided by kicking the ball over their collective heads. The elegance of these "long ball" tactics is their simplicity. It is a style that is easy to teach and does not require great tactical sophistication. The disadvantages of long-ball tactics are less obvious. Long balls are less accurate, giving opponents time to react and intercept. Long balls are often air balls that require more skill and sometimes taller players than do ground balls. Long balls played behind the defense require the attacking players to be faster than the defenders. For these reasons, the long-ball attack risks loss of possession; it is a short-lived, all-or-nothing approach. If the attack fails, the opponent quickly regains the ball. Remember, it is not only important to score, but to keep the ball so the opponents can't score.

The best tactical approach is to avoid defenders by using spaces — areas of the field where there are no opponents (Fig. 6, pg. 6).

In the space system each player must be taught how to recognize, create, and exploit space. The coach has little control after the whistle blows — plays cannot be sent in or magic performed by changing to some new offensive formation. The soccer coach's job is education — teaching players the principles of the game — how to read the game and how to respond appropriately.

Offensive Influences on Space
• Player Position
• Movement With the Ball
• Movement Without the Ball
• Passing Frequency
• Percent of Field Used in Attack

Table 2.

Space — Definitions

The first step in understanding the game of soccer is to understand what space is and its importance. Spaces are the gaps between and around opponents — areas of the field without adversaries. A player standing in such an area "has space" or "is open". A player that moves defenders from an area is "creating space". There is little risk that a player with space will lose the ball because, by definition, there aren't any opponents in the space. Good soccer teams use spaces to keep the ball, advance it, and ultimately, to score.

Usefulness of Space

Time makes space valuable. It "costs" defenders time to cross space (Fig. 3 - 5, pg. 5). Imagine a player receiving the ball with the closest opponent half a field away. It takes the defender a long time to cross the space

Figure 2 Using Space

The preferred means of advancing the ball is one with little risk. There is virtually no risk of losing the ball when large spaces are used in developing the attack. In this indoor situation, both teams are crowded into one side of the field creating a large space for safely advancing the ball.

Figure 3 Space and Time

Figure 4 Space and Time

This sequence illustrates the relationship between space and time. The amount of time a player has after receiving a ball is related to the distance of the closest defender and how rapidly that defender approaches. This player, with a relatively large amount of space, had time to control the ball, turn, look up and prepare to dribble or pass.

Figure 5 Space and Time

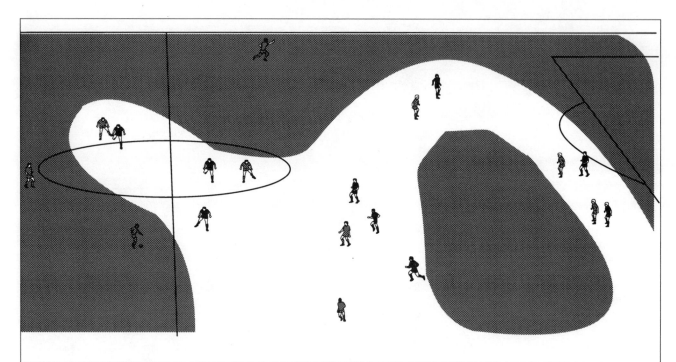

Figure 6 Changing Patterns of Space

The distribution of space (shaded) will constantly change with the movement of players and the ball. Be aware of this change. Make runs into large spaces. When covered move to create spaces. Play the ball to players running into space.

and get to the player. The amount of time depends mostly on the size of the space, but also on the speed and aggressiveness of the defender. The time is used to control the ball, advance it (Fig. 2, pg. 4) and possibly score.

Room to control a ball also makes space important — ask anyone who has tried to juggle a soccer ball in a telephone booth. The sidelines and the proximity of other players determine the space a player has. The higher one's skill level the less physical space one needs to control the ball.

Tactically, the most important thing about space is that it can be manipulated by position, movement, passing, and dribbling. These are the tools of modern offensive tactics. Decisions about dribbling, passing, shooting and moving determine the game's outcome.

Influencing Space

There is a set amount of space on each soccer field. Defenders can physically occupy only a certain portion of the field — what remains is space. The distribution of space depends entirely on the position of the defend-

Bunching at Throw-ins

In general, if attacking players spread out, defenders will spread out, too. If attackers bunch, the defenders will also bunch (Figure 7, pg. 7). These effects are most commonly seen at the time of throw-ins (see Rules page 192). Throw-ins generally attract crowds. Players gather from all over the field with the best of intentions. Potential recipients of the throw are covered, so more teammates move to help. Of course, a covering defender moves with them. Even if one player is unmarked, several defenders hover nearby, leaving no room to control the throw. If a player manages to receive and control the ball, instant pressure threatens possession. Watching the ball keeps the player from finding a safe pass recipient. If an exceptionally bright teammate were open on the far side of the field, it would be difficult to get the ball to them — the pressure would make it hard to look around, and nearby defenders would block the passing angles. This is a good example of the negative effects of bunching.

It's a different story when attackers stay dispersed at the time of a throw-in (Figure 8, pg. 7). Only three players need be in the area of the throw — one toward goal, one toward the middle of the field and one back. If the rest of the team stays spread out, most of the defenders will be scattered over the field. As a result, the player receiving the throw will have space to run, to receive the throw or to control the ball and screen it. There will be room to maneuver and find pass recipients. Chances of keeping possession are improved. Helping teammates by drawing defenders away from them indicates a high level of soccer expertise. This cooperation is called "playing off the ball".

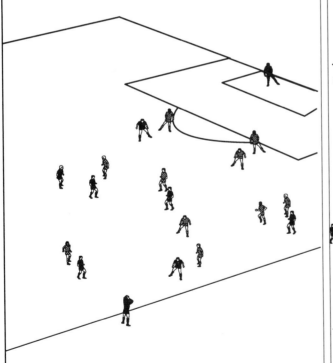

Figure 7 Bunching at Throw-ins

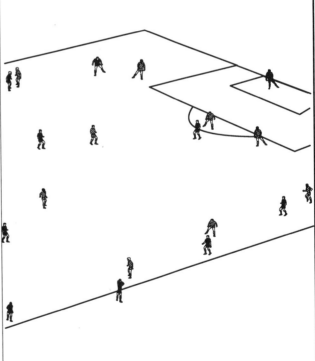

Figure 8 Spreading Out

Figure 9 Uneven Distribution of Space

The total amount of space on a soccer field does not change, only the distribution. Here, there is an uneven distribution with both teams clustered around the ball. This is a common pattern, as both teams tend to move to the ball. The spaces away from the ball are potentially useful. The problem is that players around the bunch are close together and under constant pressure. They focus on the ball and players close to it, not seeing open players in different areas. If the players are seen, it is difficult to make the long pass because of pressure and narrow passing angles. However, in this photo the player with the ball is demonstrating good vision and is taking advantage of the space. The player (#9) in the space could actually have more space by being farther away.

ers on the field (Fig. 6, pg. 6). Because they can influence the position of defenders, attackers can change the distribution of space — a process called "creating space".

An attacking team's success in manipulating space depends somewhat on skill, but mostly on the nature of the opponent's defensive system. Against a defense that uses one-on-one coverage, attackers often create space by making runs — covering defenders must follow (Fig. 11 - 13, pg. 10). In a zonal system, defenders are not so easily drawn from their areas of responsibility so attackers exploit the space between defenders.

Influencing Space 9

The area of the field also influences the defense's response to offensive tactics. Because most scores result from shots close to goal, space around goal is more valuable and more heavily protected.

The Effect of Player Positions

Defenders alter their positions based on the movements of attackers, on their team's own particular plan for defense, and on the value of the territory in question. Where the attackers are positioned is very important to the defense. If offensive players spread out over the field and the defense scatters to cover them there will be many, evenly distributed, small spaces (Fig. 8, pg. 7). This generally means less pressure near the ball, more room to maneuver, and better passing lanes. In addition, when defenders are far apart, they can't help one another effectively. Knowledge of this fact gave rise to one of the oldest coaching cries, "Spread out!" On the other hand, if the defense does not spread out to cover, attackers will have access to large amounts of space away from the defensive crowds. Either way, an attacking team seems to benefit by spreading out.

A player has a responsibility to be aware of the distribution of space, to try to manipulate it and to take advantage of it. Successful tactical play requires a team to be aware of the constantly changing distribution of space and to use an appropriate means to exploit the space that is available.

Figure 10 Creating Space by Dribbling

Dribbling or "carrying the ball with the feet" is a powerful tool for creating space. Defenders are attracted to and follow the moving ball, creating very useful space in the vacated areas behind the ball. Alert players make runs to these spaces; smart teammates get the ball to them. The run into the space from behind the ball depicted in this drawing is called an "overlap".

Figure 11 Creating Space

Space can be manipulated. Most offensive tactics are based on this fact. For example, the rationale for spreading out is that it spreads out the defense (creating space) and makes offense easier. Players often make runs in an attempt to manipulate space. This deliberate process is called "creating space".

Figure 12 Creating Space

In these photographs a player (arrow) runs at an angle from the middle of the field toward the corner. Space is created because the defender follows and is removed from an area. The player with the ball then moves into this space.

Figure 13. Creating Space

The space-creating run can be seen and justified in many ways. It is a run to fill a space and to seek offensive advantage. It is also a run to fill an open supporting position. The best movements combine all of these elements.

The Effect of Carrying the Ball

Player position is not the only factor that affects space. Player movement is also important. Defenders focus their attention on the player with the ball, often bunching around the player in possession. Defensive obsession with the ball allows the offense a chance to manipulate space. As the ball is dribbled around the field, defenders follow, creating space in the ball's wake (Fig. 10, pg. 9). Dribbling from the right side of the field to the center produces space on the right. Similarly, advancing toward the goal opens space behind the ball. This pattern is more visible with dribbling (the slowest means of advancing the ball) than with passing.

Figure 14 Creating Big Spaces

The movement of one player will usually only create a small space. To create a larger space, more players must move or concentrate in one area (as in bunches). In this indoor sequence, the movement of two attacking players shifts the entire defense, creating a very large and useful space. This space can be used to advance the ball and shoot. Unfortunately, the movements also took the defenders into a good defensive position close to goal.

Figure 15 Creating Big Spaces

The offense can use the spaces created by the moving ball, as shown by the following example: When you dribble from the sideline area to the middle, a player from behind can run into the space created (Fig. 10, pg. 9). This is an "overlap". A second example is even simpler: When dribbling toward goal you can simply drop the ball into the space behind for a trailing player to shoot. You must learn to recognize the new spaces created each time the ball moves. When properly used, these spaces can change the outcome of a game.

The Effect of Player Movements

"Appear at points that the enemy must hasten to defend; march swiftly to places where you are not expected." Sun Tzu

Many players think that when they're away from the ball, they can stop working. In fact, their main task when they're without the ball is to create space for

Figure 16 Creating Space for Oneself

Creating space for others is often a dramatic, self-sacrificing action — glorious, blistering runs are made toward the opponent's goal. In contrast, creating space for oneself is a quiet, shy, unobtrusive movement — the player simply backs up. This is an extremely difficult thing for the inexperienced player to do — it looks cowardly. However, this action is frequently essential for creating the open players upon which possession depends.

Figure 17 Creating Space for Oneself

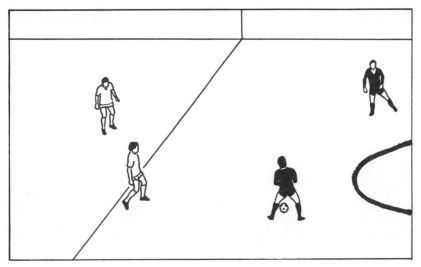

To be a total player, you must know not only when to go forward but when it is necessary to go backwards. This action is illustrated in these two figures.

Figure 18 One-Touch Passing

The ability to do one-touch passing is invaluable. Players with this level of skill can take advantage of many short-lived opportunities. This is especially valuable for scoring. In addition, one-touch passing can nullify pressure tactics and create confusion as the defense attempts to organize.

Figure 19 One-Touch Passing

This photo sequence illustrates how rapid passing creates defensive confusion and an open player. The ability to shoot rapidly is also illustrated. The goalie mishandled the ball and a goal resulted.

Figure 20 One-Touch Passing

teammates. As potential pass recipients, players without the ball also represent a threat to goal and are covered and followed by the defense (Fig. 11 - 13, pg. 10). A good player making a run toward goal may provoke a considerable defensive response. In this way, players without the ball can move defenders and "create space". Creating space makes new opportunities for the rest of the team. This unselfish action is an example of "playing off the ball".

Creating space for yourself is often more important than creating space for others. This is particularly true if you are trying to help the player with the ball (support) by creating an open passing option. While space is created for others by threatening dashes to goal, you create space for yourself by simply backing up (Fig. 16 - 17, pg. 12). This is a tough thing for most players to do, since it looks suspiciously like retreating. In the soccer world, you sometimes have to go sideways and yes, even backward before going forward. The important point is that often the simplest way to gain a little space and time is by backing up.

The Effect of Passing

Passing mesmerizes the defense in the same way dribbling does. The defense responds in the same way, by massing around the ball. Passing too long in an area increases the chance that the defensive mob drawn to the area will get the ball. Crowds always seem to favor the team without the ball. To counter the defense's tendency to bunch, the offensive team must discover and exploit the spaces that result. The ball must remain in constant motion across the width and along the length of the field (called "width and depth in attack"). This

Figure 21 Winning One-on-Ones
When an attacker goes around a defender, access is gained to space closer to goal. In addition, other defenders must move to help resulting in other open attackers. Dribbling is the most direct means of creating space. If a team dominates in the one-on-one conflicts many opportunities are created and the match will go well. Unfortunately, dominating one-on-ones is difficult — the skills are complex. In this photo a defender has just been beaten and is in the worst possible position, on the ground. A second defender must now cover.

prevents the defense from concentrating near the ball, decreasing the probability of an interception.

One ball movement that is a great advantage to teams that master it is one-touch passing. A receiver who passes the ball immediately, instead of stopping it, is completing a "one-touch" pass. By keeping the ball in constant motion, one-touch passing prevents the defense from effectively assembling around the ball, asserting pressure or tackling. Defenders become confused, frustrated. The more aggressively the defenders play, the sillier they look. They feel like the bull in a bull fight. Blind aggression becomes despair, apathy and helplessness. Teams proficient at one-touch soccer can exploit psychological and physical advantages (Fig. 18 - 20, pg. 13). They can respond to opportunities that exist for a fleeting second, including many shots and through passes. The ability to play one-touch soccer is a worthy goal for any team.

Although passing affects the distribution of space and creates space in a limited way, it is most commonly used as a tool to exploit space that exists. This space may be a natural result of the opponent's defense or be created by the team's offensive tactics. The most powerful instruments for creating this space are player movements and beating defenders.

The Effect of Beating Defenders

Beating a defender in a one-on-one is a crucial means of creating space. An attacker who beats (goes around) an opponent, gains access to the space beyond the defender (Fig. 21, pg. 14). As other defenders move to block the advancing attacker, they abandon their coverage, creating unmarked players and increasing confusion. These unmarked players are good passing options. Successful dribbling creates a more effective passing game. In addition, beating defenders has powerful psychological effects — intimidating and demoralizing opponents. Beating individual defenders by dribbling is the single most powerful offensive tool.

Skills, Tactics, Fitness & Motivation

Good tactics alone don't win games. Other factors at work include players' skills, their fitness and their motivation. These elements work in various combinations, and often a player can compensate for a deficiency in one area by developing the others. For example, a player with exceptional skills and fitness may be effective despite minor tactical deficiencies. Conversely, a player with less skill can compensate by playing very well tactically, avoiding circumstances that require a high skill level. By communicating, supporting, and creating space they help make the team a success.

Ironically, virtuoso skills often develop from poor tactical play because it exposes players to circumstances that demand high skill levels for success. Coaches increase their teams' skill levels with exercises that simulate poor tactical play, deliberately limiting space and time. The relationship between skills, tactics and fitness is fundamental to designing effective training exercises.

Fitness is important. A skilled player is unable to function when exhausted; the smart tactician is unable to use space when fatigued. Fitness affects team tactics as well, since it allows a team to use more players both on the attack and on defense. The point is this: To play soccer, you must run and run and run.

Motivation is another important aspect of soccer. All the skill, knowledge, and fitness in the world are of no value if a player sees no reason to play hard. Unmotivated players are even worse than unfit players — their potentially contagious, negative illness can infect the entire team. Unique motivations fuel each individual and each team. These factors can be recognition, avoiding disgrace (pride), revenge, material reward, fear, love, or the intrinsic satisfaction of doing something well. Strong leadership also motivates players. Creating strong motivation in players to do their best is a coaching art that depends on a coach's familiarity with the team and with each of its unique members. There are many elements to a soccer game and many ways players can contribute.

"Use each soldier according to his capabilities." Sun Tzu

Space and You

To become a better player know how much space you have and strive for more. Know which players have space. Know how your movements and the movements of others are affecting space. Good players play with their heads up — looking and analyzing space. Don't watch the ball, instead, really see the field; let the big picture dictate your actions. Being a good player also requires skills and fitness. So run and practice, practice, practice. These simple things will improve your effectiveness as a soccer player.

Photo by
Phil Stephens

17

Chapter 2

Organizing the Attack

"I must teach them to listen to each other, not just play their parts."
Leonard Bernstein

"The clever combatant looks to the effect of combined energy and does not require too much from individuals." Sun Tzu

"Apparent confusion is a product of good order; apparent weakness, of strength." Sun Tzu

Summary: In soccer's traditional system, where the players stand on the field is determined by the team's formation. Unfortunately, soccer is a dynamic game and static formations offer no conceptual basis for understanding or implementing the necessary movements. On the other hand, if a player or coach understands the game's concepts, the movements are natural and formations unnecessary.

Most of soccer's movements are based directly or indirectly on the concept of space. Movements to create or use space make possession and penetration easier. Other movements create new options and confuse the defense. Normally, the movements of support (keeping possession) have priority over all others.

The concepts and movements are the same in 2-on-2, 5-on-5 and 11-on-11, but with an increasing emphasis, in the larger games, on the activities of players away from the ball. The complex choreography that is necessary for a successful offense is dependent on a common knowledge of the game and one's teammates, good field vision and communication.

Key Concepts
• Space is used to maintain possession (support).
• Using space is the preferred method of advancing the ball.
• Players can affect the distribution of space by their position, movement, passing, and by beating defenders.
• Spreading out the defense weakens it.
• The more options available to the offense, the greater the defensive difficulty.

Table 3.

Introduction

Close your eyes during the first ten seconds of a soccer game. Open them and try to guess the formations (Fig. 22, pg. 22) that both teams use. Impossible isn't it? Formations have little to do with where players stand and move on the soccer field. A few key concepts generate most of a soccer team's complex movements. Of the five concepts (Table 3) four directly relate to space — modern soccer is a game of space and time. Formations and positions are easily replaced by an organized system of movements based on these ideas — "The Movement System".

Key Concepts

"The musical notes are only five in number but their melodies are so numerous that one cannot hear them all." Sun Tzu

Use Space to Keep Possession

A team is on offense when it is in possession of the ball. Without the ball a team cannot attack. Therefore, the actions related to keeping the ball (called "support") are a priority. A team can keep possession if a pressured player has safe passing options (supporting players). To support, a player must: 1) have adequate space; 2) be positioned along an open passing lane; and 3) be noticed (communicate). These criteria dictate the movements of the supporting players.

Use Space to Advance the Ball

"He who knows the art of the direct and the indirect approach will be victorious. Such is the art of maneuvering." Sun Tzu

Space is the focus of almost all offensive activity. Players either have space, are moving to space, or moving to create space for others. Good players constantly look, noting the evolving distribution of usable space. The ball flows from one area of space to another. When possible, the spaces are used to carry the ball toward goal. When possession is threatened, the ball moves backwards or sideways to space. Typically, the path to goal is not direct, but convoluted.

Players Can Create Space

Central to the space theory of soccer is the assumption that space can be manipulated by the attacking team. Where the attackers stand, where they move and what they do with the ball affects the arrangement of defenders and therefore — space.

Spread Out, Weaken the Defense

A defense functions more efficiently when it is compact (Fig. 63, pg. 54). When close, defenders can apply greater pressure and better assist each other by working together as a team. The defending team loses these advantages when it spreads out; becoming a loose collection of isolated, vulnerable individuals.

When spread out (Fig. 64, pg. 55), each individual attacker has more space in which to control and maneuver the ball. There are wider angles for passes and more (but smaller) spaces to probe. Individual, isolated defenders are easier to beat by dribbling and passing. It is easy to understand why "Spread out!" is a refrain almost as old as the game itself.

There are two basic methods of spreading out the defense — spreading the attacking players out and moving the ball over the entire field (called developing "width and depth" in the attack). To be most efficient, an offense should have both these elements working. Good player vision, knowledge, skill, and teamwork tie them together.

Options Make Defense Difficult

An attacking player with more options has a greater likelihood of success. The options may include passing opportunities (short, long, right, left, through or back), the option of dribbling toward goal or across the field, combination or switching plays, and shooting. The availability of these oppor-

---

The Movement System Rules

When not to move (See page 36)

- If you already have space where you can receive the ball
- If you are keeping a covering defender from making an important defensive contribution

When to move

- If above conditions aren't met

Basic movements

- Move to create basic passing options (right, left, through)
- Sprint to space after passing (see page 30)
- Make runs to spaces where you can receive the ball
- Move to fill spaces created when players run forward
- When covered, move to create space for others
- Move to confuse or distract defenders

Timing of movements (See page 30)

- Any movement with the expectation of receiving a pass must be coordinated with the player holding the ball

Cycling (See page 35)

- Players behind or at the same level as the ball make runs forward
- Covered players in front of the ball and in the goal area make crossfield runs to create space, then move to fill gaps at the back created by players running forward

Bunching prevention

- Keep only three or four players in the vicinity of the ball (right, left, through, back)
- Stay at least 10 yards apart whenever possible.
- When covered near the ball, move to create space

Table 4.

Movement Details

Movements of Players Close to the Ball

- Move to create left and right (square) passing options for anyone receiving the ball.
- Square players stay to the side of and behind the ball (normal position). (See Fig. 27, pg. 26)
- With the ball at the field edge, one square player is "downline" (See Fig. 25, pg. 25).
- When there are six feet between the ball and the field edge, the square player is to the side of and behind the ball.
- If a square player is not covered they may be even with or ahead of the ball. The position of the defender at the ball determines how far downfield the square player can move. (See Fig. 28, pg. 26)
- Players positioned in the center of the field always make a run downline if they are covered and the ball is along the sidelines. This run may be "in front of" or "behind" the ball. (See Fig. 26, pg. 25)
- A square player, properly positioned behind the ball, will sprint through or run to a new space if covered. Other players should be alert to fill this position. (See Fig. 29, pg. 26)

- After right and left passing options are created, through players try to get open closer to goal. (See Fig. 30, pg. 27)

Basic Combination Plays

- If the player with the ball dribbles toward a teammate, that player should move toward and behind them by switching or doing a take-over. Do not run away or back up! (See Fig. 45, pg. 39)
- If the defender at the ball is close, aggressive or slow and there is space behind the defender, a teammate should move to set up a wall pass. (See Fig. 56, pg. 48)
- Three player combinations have similar requirements to wall passes — a beatable defender with space behind them. However, a third player takes part. (See Fig. 51–53, pg. 46)

Players Away From the Ball

- Find a space where you can receive the ball. (See Fig. 30, pg. 27)
- If covered, draw defender as far from center or from the ball as possible or move to create space.

Table 5.

tunities depends on the player's individual skill and the tactical resources of the team. At minimum, the attacking team tries to offer left, right and through passing options to the player with the ball. With each additional option the defensive job becomes more difficult and the prospect of offensive success greater.

Creating a System of Play

Ideally, organizational systems should provide specific guidelines for player position and movement, and encourage the creation and use of space. The objective of an organizational system is the efficient creation and use of space to maintain possession, advance the ball, and score. Theoretically, there are probably an infinite number of ways eleven players could be organized on a field. The organizational structure may be a geometric formation of players, a system of rules for player movement, or a collection of commonly understood concepts. In soccer, the formation system has had a monopoly for over 80 years, with little thought given to alternate approaches.

The Traditional Approach

Early soccer had little organization. The two sides simply agreed on some basic rules — such as the number of players each side would have, what the boundaries were, and what constituted a "goal". At first the teams were merely unruly mobs, running wildly about chasing and kicking the ball. Without skill, discipline or tactics, the game looked similar to games played by beginning teams anywhere. As the sport evolved, the rules became standardized and leagues formed. The game changed — teams became interested in improving their chances of winning through organization and tactics.

Passing was a breakthrough discovery and spreading out was the key to using it. Using passes, the mob could be easily avoided, the ball easily advanced and goals scored. The simplest way to spread out the team was to assign each player an area of the field in which to play. The resulting pattern of players was the team's "formation". Although initially distributed in one or two lines across the field, three lines became standard (Fig. 22 & 23, pg. 22). Attacking players were in the first line, players with mixed responsibilities in the second, and defenders in the third. The formation's name came from the number of players in each row, starting with the defenders. For example, a 4-4-2 formation had four defenders, four middle players (midfielders, halfbacks or links) and two forwards (strikers).

As our understanding of the game has evolved, so has our view of the role of formations. From the modern perspective, formations only help keep the attacking team spread out. They don't provide precise guidelines concerning where to stand or where to move — in fact, they restrict movement. Movements only tend to break up the orderly formation and create confusion. Because formations hamper movement they also inhibit the optimal creation and utilization of space. For these reasons, the formation system of organization is outdated and needs replacement. The movement system is one attractive alternative.

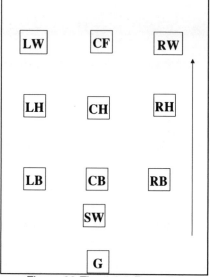

Figure 22 The 4-3-3 Formation
Players in a formation are arrayed in three lines — usually with an extra player behind the defenders, the sweeper (**SW**). There are three defenders (**B**acks), three midfielders (**H**alfbacks) and three forwards (two **W**ings and a **C**enter **F**orward). The letters come from the row and whether the player is on the **R**ight, **L**eft or in the **C**enter. **G** is the Goalkeeper.

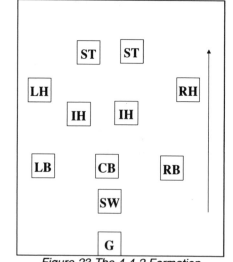

Figure 23 The 4-4-2 Formation
The 4-4-2 uses two **I**nside **H**alfbacks but has only two full-time forwards (**ST**rikers). The left & right halfback have a more offensive role. The strikers and halfbacks are given much greater freedom of movement in this system.

To Support, A Player Must:
• Have adequate space
• Be positioned where the ball can be easily passed
• Be noticed

Table 6.

Offensive Processes & Movement
Possession (Support)
• Creating left & right passing options
• Adjusting movements of square players
• Moving to create space when covered
Penetration
• Moving to space after passing
• Running to spaces behind defense
• Movements of through players to find space where the ball can be passed
Creating New Opportunities
• All movements are useful
• Moving crossfield

Table 7.

The Movement System

"In the tumult and uproar the battle seems chaotic, but there is no disorder; the troops appear to be milling about in circles but cannot be defeated." Sun Tzu

"The Movement System" is a form of "total football" — not using formations or positions. Movement rules provide the organizational structure. (Tables 4 & 5). These rules are based on the concepts of space outlined in Table 3. At its simplest, the system consists of three primary sets of movements: 1) movements to create left and right passing options for the ball; 2) movements after passing and; 3) movements into space or to create space. A more detailed accounting lists the movements this way: 1) movements related to support (including creating basic options and adjusting movements); 2) movements after passing; 3) movements to create or fill space; 4) movements to confuse defensive markings; and 5) movements that bring players back to fill gaps created by others moving forward.

The movement system has many advantages. Because it is concept based, it is easier to understand — very specific, logical instruction can be offered. It provides a theoretical basis for game evaluation. Players find it more enjoyable to play because they know what they are doing, can improvise, and work together more as a team. The system increases player efficiency and creativity. The team is more successful because players know what they are doing and the tremendous increase in movements usually totally disrupts a traditional, position-oriented defense.

Offensive Processes and the Movement System

There are three basic offensive processes: 1) keeping possession; 2) penetration and; 3) creating new opportunities. Soccer movements can be conveniently organized and discussed using these processes (Table 7).

Keeping Possession

Support is helping the player with the ball by providing safe passing options. Supporting players, like all players, are trying to have space in an area where they can receive the ball. The "supporting players" are just closer to the ball, usually within 10 to 15 yards. More formally, supporting players must: 1) have space; 2) have a clear passing lane to the ball; and 3) communicate. The basic process involves always providing a player with space to the left and right of the person with the ball.

Support uniquely combines many concepts of the movement system. The process involves creating passing options, moving to find space, and moving to create space for others. Many subtler nuances, such as staying spread out and adjusting one's position to maintain a passing lane, also apply.

Creating passing options is an important factor in good support. The player with the ball should have a supporting player to either side (Fig. 24, pg. 25). Having two options makes the defender's job more difficult. These right and left supporting players, called "square players", are usually positioned at an angle behind the ball (Fig. 27, pg. 26).

A supporting player should have enough space to control the ball, get their head up and look around for several seconds. To get these five seconds of time without defensive pressure is difficult and requires much space. To find this space, a supporting player generally must be positioned at an angle behind the player with the ball. A supporting player must often back away from covering defenders to get this space (Fig. 16, pg. 12). Only when totally unmarked, or when the defenders are playing extremely loosely will the supporting player be even with or ahead of the ball (Fig. 28, pg. 26).

A supporting player must be accessible — positioned along a clear passing lane. The supporting player must not get cut off by the defender marking the ball or by any intervening defenders. Thus, the supporting player must adjust their position not only to keep adequate space, but also to be in an open passing lane. A player positioned behind the ball usually has space and is accessible.

Although the square players try to be 10 yards from the player with the ball, this isn't always possible near the sidelines or corners. In these circumstances the boundaries force the square players closer to the ball.

Talking is an important part of support. Supporting players must communicate whenever the player with the ball has their head down or isn't aware of their presence.

When square players are unsuccessful at finding sufficient space or unable to remain accessible they run to create space (Fig. 29, pg. 26). Running away from the ball when support is needed is difficult; it requires faith in one's teammates. Another teammate, aware of the constant need to have both passing options, must immediately move to fill the space created. Most frequently,

Mistakes in Support
Fig. 31 to 35

- Incomplete supporting group
- Filling through before square
- Supporting players too close
- Square players too far downfield
- Too many players in a position
- Not moving when covered
- Not sprinting through after passing.

Table 8.

Figure 24 Supporting Group

Players move to create left and right passing options (square) for anyone receiving the ball. The position and movement of these square players is dictated by the need to help the player with the ball. To support properly, these players must have space in an area where they can receive the ball. After square players are in place, others seek open positions closer to goal.

Figure 25 Downline Position

When the player with the ball is along the sidelines, one square player is "downline".

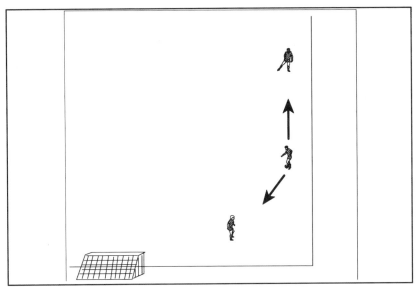

Figure 26 Moving Downline

Players positioned in the center of the field always make a run "downline" if they are covered and the ball is along the sidelines. This may be "in front of" or "behind" the ball.

Figure 27 Square!

The exact position of the square players is a controversial subject. The only thing that really matters is that they have space and a clear passing lane. To achieve these "criteria" it is frequently necessary to be positioned at an angle behind the ball, as illustrated here.

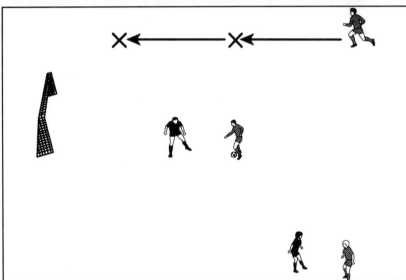

Figure 28 Moving Up

If a square player is not covered they may be even with or ahead of the ball. The position of the defender at the ball determines how far downfield they can move. Remember, the normal position of the square player is at an angle behind the player with the ball.

Figure 29 Creating Space Square

A square player, properly positioned behind the ball, will sprint through or run to a new space if covered (arrows 1 & 2). Other players should be alert to fill this position.

Figure 30 Through Players

After both square positions are filled we try to move someone into a through position. This can be done in several ways, including shifting a square player through and moving another person to their vacated position. The through players, like all players, try to find a space where they can receive the ball. This means carefully watching the passing lanes of the person with the ball. Through players often can't find much space but they still try to position themselves where they can receive a pass.

Figure 31 Mistakes in Support

In this photo the entire team has "gone for goal" leaving no support for the ball. To get the ball to a teammate, the player with the ball must beat a defender. What if he loses the ball? The attackers near goal should move to support the player with the ball and try to spread out the defense, creating useful space near the goal.

Figure 32 Mistakes in Support

Possession is the foundation of all offensive activity. Therefore, we support square (a position helpful to possession) before we run to a through position (a position of penetration). The offensive player currently standing through should move downline, to a position square along the boards. This movement also can be seen as a run to space or a run to create space in the middle.

Figure 33 Mistakes in Support

Both the square players in this situation are caught making a common mistake — creeping downfield. In this case there is no harm done as there is no pressure on the player with the ball. When the defender at the ball gets close the square players must be accessible. Frequently, this means being at an angle behind the player with the ball. Creeping downfield is bad for three reasons: 1) the angle for square passes is narrow, risking interception, 2) the square players will have less space, and 3) it decreases through space, putting more defenders close to goal.

through players move back to fill these spaces. To happen in a timely manner, this process demands team vision and alertness.

For a team to be successful, all supporting activities — creating options, keeping space, maintaining a passing lane, communicating, and creating space, must happen quickly and naturally. The most common mistakes are listed in Table 8. Without good support, possession and offense are not possible.

Penetration

To penetrate the defense means to advance the ball toward goal. This can be done by dribbling or by passing. Movements related to penetration include creating the through passing option, running to space, and creating space. When possible, we try to penetrate the defense by advancing the ball in areas

Figure 34 Mistakes in Support

When covered move! The easiest and simplest way to get open is to back up. Don't worry about backing up too far. If the defender follows, room is created for easy through passes. Here, the ball is being passed back to the goalie because of inadequate support. The square player to the right of the ball could have backed up. The left square player didn't back up either — just took off downfield. Many players will panic in this situation and kick the ball blindly downfield. The correct pass is to the goalie.

Figure 35 Mistakes in Support

This is a very common mistake. In this situation, the dark-shirted square player is moving toward the ball. Bad! This guy must have only one oar in the water. Look at the tremendous space he would have if he were in the middle. He would be in a very good position to run at goal or shoot. Do you notice another mistake? Someone could be making a run to increase the space in the middle.

where there are no defenders — called spaces. This strategy includes difficult passes to players running into spaces behind the defense (Fig. 57, pg. 48). These spaces are "discovered" behind beatable defenders or deliberately created by player movements. When usable space is not available, we must use more skill and advance the ball against defensive resistance. Lastly, in extreme circumstances, we may resort to playing long balls into the area in front of the goal.

The most common means of penetration is the through pass. After creating right and left square passing options player(s) move to create passing options closer to goal (Fig. 30, pg. 27); provided those movements won't place them in an offsides position. Defensive efforts to prevent passes to the through players result in more space for the square (supporting) players. In effect, the threat of penetration makes possession easier. Conversely, defensive efforts to deny possession by closer marking of the square players, increase the space behind the defense, creating increased opportunities for penetration.

The attacking team continually seeks to penetrate the defense by sprinting to goal after passing. This essential movement starts many combination plays. After any square or through pass a covered player should sprint to space (Fig. 37, pg. 31). Running after making a pass is optional when unmarked and shouldn't be done if your pass will be intercepted (Fig. 36, pg. 31). There are two types of runs made after passing — toward goal, the most common, or runs behind the player receiving the ball (overlaps) (Fig. 39, pg. 32). The space available dictates the direction of the run. If there is a through space, sprint to it. If there is space on the other side of the pass recipient, move to that.

Spontaneous, penetrating runs to space (not after passing), made with the intention of receiving a pass, requires timing and coordination between two players (Fig. 57, pg. 48). The run must be made when the player with the ball has their head up (Fig. 110, pg. 94) and after eye contact is made, or the run won't be seen. The actual call for the ball is the sudden acceleration toward the space. This catches the attention of the player with the ball and triggers the pass. Careful timing is critical, especially if being offsides is a consideration.

Runs into space are commonly along a curved path, as if the player making the run were tied by a long rope to the ball (Fig. 60, pg. 49). A player making such a curved run can continuously see the ball and is accessible for a pass during most of the run. Many of these runs have a dual purpose — to beat the defense and get the ball, or to create space.

The timing of a run to create space is not as critical; but, there are other considerations. Runs made to create space are better if they draw the defense's attention. A dramatic sprint to goal will be more effective than a casual trot. Runs toward goal are of greater concern to the defense and are more effective than runs in other directions. Unfortunately, these runs compress the defense into the goal area — something undesirable. Runs made from the goal area to the sides and crossfield runs produce more useful space, but are less effective.

Creating New Opportunities

If, in our quest to penetrate the defense, there are no good options, it is time to do things that will reshuffle the defense, creating confusion and new opportunities. Switching (Fig. 48, pg. 44), combination plays (Fig. 47 & 51 to 53, pg. 46), changing the field of play (Fig. 65, pg. 56), stretching the defense (Fig. 64, pg. 55), attacking individual defenders (Fig. 21, pg. 14), and pass-move combinations (Fig. 37 to 39, pg. 32) accomplish this.

All movements have the potential of creating new opportunities — including the basic movements to create left and right passing options. Because all movements have this potential, it is important to "structure in" as many movements as possible and to encourage other spontaneous movements. Coaches "structure in" movements by requiring them of players. Examples of this are

Figure 36 Pass But Don't Move?

A movement (run) after passing is optional if you are unmarked, if the pass recipient needs immediate support, or if the pass is going to be intercepted.

Figure 37 Pass and Run to Space

The most common run after a square pass is to a through space where a return pass can be made. If the pass isn't forthcoming the player continues the run, moving to a supporting position on the other side of the ball. This run is the beginning of many successful combination plays, particularly wall passes. Teammates must move to fill the space created by this run.

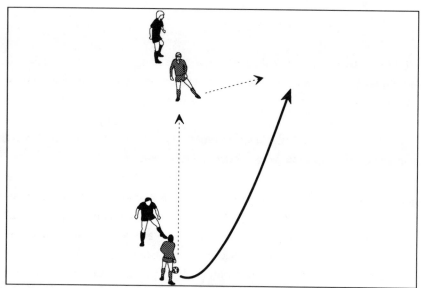

Figure 38 Through Pass, Sprint to Space

This is similar to the movement described above but starts with a through pass.

Figure 39 Pass and Follow

A run behind the pass recipient is made if space is available on the other side of the pass recipient.

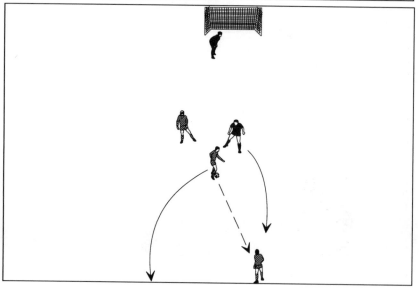

Figure 40 Back Pass and Support

A player that makes a back pass must move to support that player. Never abandon a teammate.

Body Language

The need for communication arises from two facts — people can't read other people's minds and people do not have eyes on the back of their heads. Warnings, intentions, advice, and encouragement are all communicated verbally. Communication is something that must be encouraged and practiced. The soccer field can never be a silent place.

Seventy percent of communication is non-verbal. We suggest more with our posture, gestures and facial expressions than we do with our words. In soccer this is also true. We communicate our intentions by our head position, facial expressions, by the direction we are facing and by where we position the ball (Fig. 41, pg. 34).

Pointing is a useful communication tool in soccer — it is silent, quick and precise. When a player starts to run behind a defender and points to a spot, it is clear where they are going and where the ball should be passed.

A player with their head down is not signalling a pass, but is likely to dribble or shoot. Attackers and defenders read this body language and respond accordingly. The defense concentrates on the player with the ball, often double-teaming. Coverage away from the ball is relaxed. Attacking teammates move to improve dribbling chances or prepare for a shot. If the player is in danger of losing the ball, support and verbal communication become essential.

The direction a player is facing or moving with the ball also sends a message. Facing the goal is an aggressive stance implying a desire to penetrate the defense by dribbling or passing. A teammate, seeing this, can position for a through pass, make a run to create space for dribbling, or move to set up a combination play.

A player that is turned sideways with respect to the covering defender has assumed a more defensive posture. This is not a position suitable for penetrating the defense by dribbling. Through passes and combination plays are possible, but often this stance is used to protect the ball. What the player frequently needs is a good, open, safe passing opportunity (support).

An attacker that is completely turned with a defender on their back is generally signalling for help. However, a good player, capable of keeping possession under pressure may be looking to play the ball square to players running forward.

Other subtle clues to a player's intentions include how close the ball is to their body and its angle with respect to the direction the person is facing. A player that is going to kick the ball a long distance with the instep shoves the ball away and to the side. With an inside-of-the foot pass, a line can be drawn between the passer, the ball and the target. When intending to dribble, the ball is kept close to the feet.

Although all these things are common knowledge among soccer players, they are not totally reliable because they are also used as fakes. A good player will constantly reposition the ball and send out false information about their intentions. With good players, body language can be a weapon of deception.

Figure 41 Body Language

Seventy percent of human communication is non-verbal body language. Intentions are communicated not just by words but by gestures, head position, positioning of the ball, posture and even by the direction one faces. These same elements can be used to deceive opponents. In this photo, the player with the ball is telling us by ball position, posture and head position, that he will make an inside-of-the-foot pass to someone to his right. A lot has been said without uttering a word. Also, notice the total lack of support.

Figure 42 The Situation Talks

Game situations talk to smart players. On offense it makes combination plays possible, on defense it helps players intercept passes. The white-shirted player in the center sees the aggressive defender approaching the ball and the space in the corner — wall pass time. He is moving into position to be the wall. His open-handed (give-me) gesture indicates a desire for the ball and a willingness to make the return pass.

requiring left and right passing options and requiring movements after passing. Spontaneous movements that create new opportunities include cross-field movements without the ball, runs to create space and runs to space.

Movement Priorities

Certain movements are more important than others. Supporting movements have the highest priority. The team must always create right and left passing options for the player with the ball (Fig. 24, pg. 25). These players must adjust their positions to provide the best support, assuring continued possession.

"What do I do when my team has the ball?" First, and every time someone new gets the ball, check to see if they have close right and left passing options (For information on what you do with the ball, see Chapter 3). If they don't, or if one of these "square" players takes off, move to fill the open position. If there are square players on either side of the ball check for a teammate closer to goal. If there isn't one, go there (provided it won't put you offsides). One player per square and through position, please. The square and through players make adjusting movements outlined in Fig. 24 to 30, pg. 25.

For information on what to do when the player with the ball moves forward or across the field check Fig. 44 to 46, pg. 38.

If you are not in the group around the ball, you have three primary functions: stretch the defense by staying spread out, create space for other teammates by making runs, or make runs into spaces where you can receive the ball. You must decide whether you can do the most good by simply staying wide or deep and stretching the defense, by making a run to create a space or making a run into space. It will depend on the game situation. Watch your teammates; their movements create spaces for you to run into or for you to fill if they are made at the team's rear.

Movements after passing are next in priority. Players should sprint to space after passing. This is usually to a space closer to goal (Fig. 38, pg. 32) but it may be an overlapping run to a space in a square position (Fig. 39, pg. 32). These runs have three functions — to penetrate the defense, to create defensive confusion and to create space near the ball for support. Also, sprinting to space after passing suggests wall passes, forcing defenders to play looser, decreasing pressure.

Filling the spaces created by these runs is the next priority. This usually . requires players in front of the ball to come back (Fig. 29, pg. 26).

Sprints to space are next in importance. Observe the passing lanes of the player with the ball. If there is space along a lane, look for the opportunity to make a run to that space (Fig. 57, pg. 48).

Runs to create space (Fig. 11 to 13, pg. 10) and to confuse the defense (Fig. 48, pg. 44) have lower priority. However, these runs may become very important in a close contest between sophisticated teams.

The Movement Cycle

"For they end and recommence; cyclical, as are the movements of the sun and moon. They die away and are reborn; recurrent, as are the passing seasons." Sun Tzu

The casual observer sees the movements in a good soccer game as chaotic and random. In fact, on most teams they are. However, they can be structured, purposeful and cyclic (Fig. 43, pg. 37). The cycle has three phases that restart with each pass. Uncompleted cycles overlap like waves from many pebbles thrown into a pond. The three phases in each cycle are 1) structured movements; 2) unstructured exploitation movements; and 3) recovery movements.

The structured movements in the first phase include — movements to create passing options around the ball, adjusting movements by the supporting players, movements made after passing, and movements away from the ball to create space. These movements create a swirl of activity resulting in space that is used in the second phase.

In the second phase, players make runs into the spaces created. Players coming from behind the ball often make these runs, carefully coordinating them so they will be seen and a pass delivered.

In the third phase, the team seeks to recover from any imbalances created by these movements. The team spreads out to cover the width of the field and fills any gaps created by the runs. Some refer to this recovery process as "balance" or "restoring balance". It is a process requiring good vision and unselfish teamwork.

When Not To Move

The old saying, "When covered, move!" is still good advice. However, there are times when you shouldn't move. A good player must learn these exceptions. The rationale for not moving is that a defender may be making a mistake by covering you. The defender could be in a better position and contributing substantially more to their team's successful defense.

The best example of this is when you are being covered while positioned behind your teammate with the ball (Fig. 55, pg. 48). Defenders generally try to strengthen the defense by being between the ball and the goal — every additional defender between the ball and goal makes successful penetration less likely. By covering you, there are fewer defenders goal-side and the defense is weaker. When tightly covered far from the ball, the situation is similar. Any movement toward goal may only put the defender in a better defensive position (Fig. 49 & 50, pg. 45). Therefore, covered players behind the ball don't make runs to create space. Players, when covered far from the ball, make fewer runs to create space than those close to the ball. This awareness of how your position is affecting others is an example of "playing without the ball" or "playing off the ball" (See Box Text pg. 36).

Movement Choreography

Soccer is like ballet. There are many complex movements that must be precisely coordinated to achieve a successful performance. It is a cycle in which the activities of the player with the ball greatly affect the movements of players away from the ball. Those movements in turn will affect the next action of the player with the ball. Each player must understand how what they do will affect what others can do and contribute to or detract from the team's total achievement.

The Movement Effects of Dribbling to Goal

The natural inclination of players receiving the ball is to get their head down, and take off (Fig. 44, pg. 38). This is usually bad, because when a player

---

Playing Off the Ball

A one word synonym for playing off the ball would be teamwork. Playing off the ball includes everything a player can do when they don't have the ball to help others on the team. It includes supporting, creating options, creating space, making runs to space, confusing the defense, distracting the defense, stretching the defense and communicating.

These are not the types of things that are appreciated by the average coach, teammate or fan, but they are the types of things that make a successful team. Many good coaches know that it is not only what a player does with the ball, but the things that they do without the ball, that determine greatness.

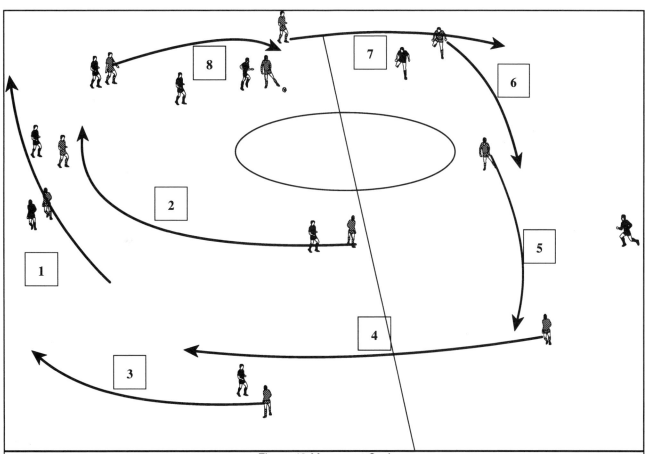

Figure 43 Movement Cycle

Both structured (e.g., creating right and left passing options, passing and moving) and spontaneous movements (e.g., runs to space) have the potential of creating new spaces. These runs create a cascade of additional movements (a cycle) as players successively respond to the actions of their teammates. This figure depicts examples of the cycle. Movement 1 is a spontaneous movement of a covered player to create space. Movement 2 is a response to the space created. If this player is unsuccessful in beating the defender or receiving a pass he continues, dragging the covering defender to further enhance the space. Movement 3 is a similar movement of a covered attacker to space. Movement 4 is a movement with great potential. An attacker coming from behind the ball is often unmarked and surprises the defense. All the movements to space (2, 3, 4) should be made when a pass is possible and the passer sees the movement. These movements to space will often create a very unbalanced player distribution, with all the players on one side. This could be a problem if there was a sudden turnover. As a result, players move to fill gaps at the back (5). Other players also compensate, moving back from the crowded areas of the field, redistributing the team (6, 7 and 8).

dribbles it discourages movements by players away from the ball. The dribbling player usually has their head down, creating extreme tunnel vision. Runs will not be seen so they are not made. With a rapidly advancing player other players struggle just to keep up — with little time for more creative crossfield or space creating runs. The most players can hope to do is assist the dribbling player by moving defenders from their path, setting up a wall pass, or positioning for a shot or centering pass. Because of their head-down position, any communication with these players must be verbal. For these reasons, resist the impulse to take off every time you receive the ball. A wiser course is to stop the ball, look up and pass.

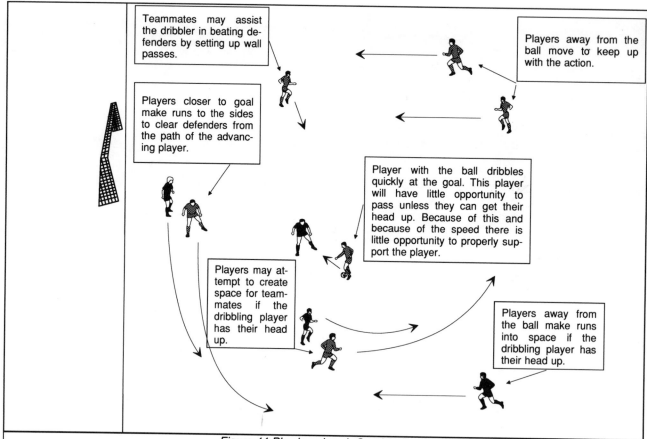

Teammates may assist the dribbler in beating defenders by setting up wall passes.

Players away from the ball move to keep up with the action.

Players closer to goal make runs to the sides to clear defenders from the path of the advancing player.

Player with the ball dribbles quickly at the goal. This player will have little opportunity to pass unless they can get their head up. Because of this and because of the speed there is little opportunity to properly support the player.

Players may attempt to create space for teammates if the dribbling player has their head up.

Players away from the ball make runs into space if the dribbling player has their head up.

Figure 44 Plowing ahead, Good or Bad?

When you get the ball do you feel obliged to take the ball as far downfield as you can, passing only as a last resort? Fight the urge! You should dribble only when you are in a large open space, when there is but a single defender to beat for a shot on goal, and when there are no passing options. Plowing straight ahead is usually dumb. Your teammates have to run just to keep up, leaving no time to set up wall passes, make creative crossfield runs or runs to space. Also dribbling players usually have tunnel vision and can't see what their teammates are doing anyway. In most circumstances, the best thing is to look and plan before you get the ball, then control the ball, get your head up, look again, and pass. By playing more slowly and deliberately you give your teammates chances to make runs and give yourself the opportunity to see them and make the most accurate pass.

The Movement Effects of Crossfield Dribbling

Dribbling crossfield is one of the most productive things a player can do (Fig. 45, pg. 39). It causes many defensive problems and makes opportunities for creative combination plays. A player dribbles crossfield: 1) to switch the play to open players on the other side of the field; 2) to get in better position for a shot and; 3) to leave an area where there are few passing or dribbling opportunities. It is easier for a player dribbling crossfield to keep their head up because the ball isn't exposed; it is shielded by their body. A heads-up player can see passing opportunities and therefore teammates make runs.

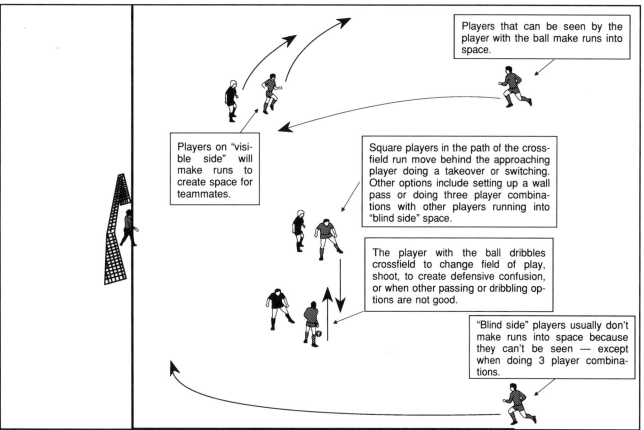

Players that can be seen by the player with the ball make runs into space.

Players on "visible side" will make runs to create space for teammates.

Square players in the path of the crossfield run move behind the approaching player doing a takeover or switching. Other options include setting up a wall pass or doing three player combinations with other players running into "blind side" space.

The player with the ball dribbles crossfield to change field of play, shoot, to create defensive confusion, or when other passing or dribbling options are not good.

"Blind side" players usually don't make runs into space because they can't be seen — except when doing 3 player combinations.

Figure 45 Crossfield Creativity

Players that only run toward goal are like artists trying to paint pictures using only vertical lines. To create art requires an infinite variety of lines — vertical, horizontal, angled, and curved. Similarly, to create soccer art requires more than runs toward goal. Dribbling across the field is an example of a more creative run. Dribble crossfield when it is difficult to go forward, when you see space on the other side, when you don't have a good passing option or when you don't have anything better to do. Crossfield runs surprise and confuse defenders. It is difficult for defenders to stop a crossfield run so it is a good way to get a shot on goal. Running crossfield often takes you directly toward teammates. Instead of backing up or running away they should run behind you — switching or doing a takeover. Get your head up as you cross the field. Look for teammates making runs into space. Crossfield dribbling runs are creative, productive and under-utilized. Show your soccer creativity and make it a part of your style of play.

Players in the path of the crossfield run should not back up or run away, but move toward and behind the approaching ball carrier. This crossing of paths creates the opportunity for a takeover or a simple switching maneuver — both confuse the opponents. A square player in the path of the run also can set up a wall pass or a three-player combination play with players making runs on the "blind side" (behind) the approaching player. Players farther from the ball on the "visible side" can make runs into space or to create space. If you have the inclination to get the ball and take off dribbling, consider the crossfield run — it has many advantages.

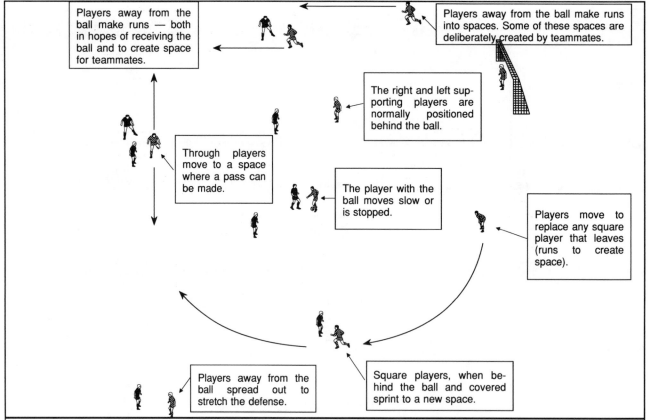

Players away from the ball make runs — both in hopes of receiving the ball and to create space for teammates.

Players away from the ball make runs into spaces. Some of these spaces are deliberately created by teammates.

The right and left supporting players are normally positioned behind the ball.

Through players move to a space where a pass can be made.

The player with the ball moves slow or is stopped.

Players move to replace any square player that leaves (runs to create space).

Players away from the ball spread out to stretch the defense.

Square players, when behind the ball and covered sprint to a new space.

Figure 46 Stop And Look, The Best Thing To Do?

Do the best players make things happen? Sometimes the best players let things happen. The best players are "heads-up", poised, cool under pressure, and patient. Develop the habit of constantly looking and the habit of planning. Show patience by controlling the ball, getting your head up and looking. Often you will have time to wait — use it. When you wait, it encourages your teammates to make runs to space. You can see them because your angle of vision is greatest when stopped. You can hit them with a pass because your passing accuracy is greatest when stopped. Learn these things and others will begin to recognize you as one of the best.

Movements with the Ball Stopped or Moving Slowly

Usually when a player receives the ball, they should simply control it, get their head up and pass (Fig. 46, pg. 40). This is the default playing style — two-touch. This is preferred because the player will have the greatest ability to see passing opportunities. Because their activities may be rewarded by a good pass, players away from the ball are more likely to make runs into space and to create space. Other runs will be made to support the ball by creating left and right (square) passing options. Players close to goal will work to find an open space where they can receive a pass. Stopping or moving slowly with the head up, encourages the greatest amount of "playing off the ball".

There are several other reasons for stopping or advancing slowly with the head up. First, ball control is greater, thus fewer turnovers. Also, a player can make

Teaching "Total Football"

A team that intends to play "total football" should never use positions in practice. The emphasis should be on the universal player with no segregation of players into strikers, midfielders and defenders. All players participate equally in all exercises. Small games are the principle teaching vehicle.

Movements are taught in the order of their priority. They are taught by restrictions (e.g., requiring sprints to goal after passing), by special games (4 vs. 2 keep-away to show the relation between square and through players) and by coaching input during exercises. Simple exercises such as three vs. one keep-away can be used to teach the habit of creating the basic passing options. More options can be added with other small games.

Movements after passing are introduced with the use of restrictions. Two effective restrictions are: 1) Sprint to space after passing and 2) Overlap the pass recipient. Balancing movements to fill the gaps created by these runs must be taught at the same time.

Recognizing and timing runs to space are best taught with two-vs.-two keep-away. Movements to create space are taught in a stepwise fashion. Chalktalk precedes walk-through field demonstrations. Three player combination drills in which a player makes a run to create space can be used as the first practical applications. The last step is to have small-sided games with 5 or more players with an emphasis on creating useful spaces.

Smaller games are best for teaching skill, support, combination play, and simple penetration methods. Larger sides emphasize organization, field vision, and playing off the ball. The progression to larger-sided games must be gradual. In this transition, it is particularly important to emphasize vision and how players away from the ball contribute.

Intrasquad scrimmages and scrimmages against other teams are essential to build confidence in the system. A five-a-side tournament with a friendly rival is a good introductory event. Ultimately, the team must gain experience with full-sided scrimmages.

the most accurate passes when stopped or going slowly. Lastly, the "head-up" position may back-off nearby defenders. The "head-down" position has just the opposite effect — attracting defenders like sharks to fresh blood. Often the best thing to do with the ball is the easiest — stop, get your head up and pass.

Compromise Systems

It is difficult for most coaches to go to a system of total football. For these coaches, compromise systems can be devised. One compromise would be simply to retain a single player for defensive organization and prevention of gaps at the back — a sweeper. A second possible compromise would be to have the six attacking players play total football, but also to keep three traditional defenders and a sweeper.

A third possibility is to have the players near the ball use the movement rules discussed previously, while players farther from the ball stay in territories dictated by a traditional formation. This option uses two groups: the square, through and back players players around the ball; and a traditional formation for the other 5 or 6 players. The positions around the ball are given priority because of the importance of possession. That is, if there is a square position open, somebody should come and fill it. This system improves a team's support and combination play, but it doesn't reap the benefits of total football with its many spontaneous movements, crossfield runs, and runs to space.

Converting to total football takes an act of faith. The conversion requires time and patience. You must start out slowly, with small-sided games. If your approach is, "OK team. Today we are going to play 11-on-11 total football," you will fail.

Practical Applications

Combination Plays

Simple combination plays are synchronized moving and passing combinations executed by two or three players. Perhaps the most commonly recognized example is the wall pass. Other examples include simple switching plays, through passes to space and the more complex three player combinations. Combination plays beat defenders, create confusion or simply reshuffle the defense.

The common element in all combination plays is space. Combination plays exploit space. It is recognition of the space that allows coordinated passing and running without a spoken word.

Most combination plays require more than the recognition of space to be successful. The player running into the space must beat a defender. Inattentive, aggressive or tight-marking defenders are most easily beaten. In three-player combinations, two players, by passing and moving, can disguise the third player's run.

Combination plays are spontaneous yet structured — dependent on the ability of the players to recognize the proper context for their occurrence. Here lies a great coaching challenge — to expand a team's repertoire of combination plays.

Wall Pass

The wall pass is soccer's oldest combination play. The player with the ball beats a defender by using a teammate, like a wall, to bounce the ball behind the defender (Fig. 47, pg. 43). Attempt a wall pass when the following elements exist: 1) there is a beatable defender at the ball; 2) there is a sufficiently large space behind that defender; 3) there is a teammate properly positioned to act as the "wall"; and 4) both players recognize the situation.

The player with the ball passes to the "wall" and sprints to the space behind the defender to receive a return pass. The defender at the ball should be beatable. The usual beatable defender is marking too closely. Other beatable defenders are slow, approaching too fast, or ball watching. The attacker also can make a passive defender beatable (too close) by dribbling at them to decrease the space.

The first pass should be made to the feet of the player positioned as the wall, using the inside-of-the-foot pass (push pass) because of its consistent accuracy. The wall player should be even with the defender marking at the ball. The distance of the wall player from the ball varies with the size of the space into which the return pass must be played. If this space is small, the wall player must be closer to play the ball more quickly. The wall player faces the ball. The "give-me" gesture (hands down, palms forward) is a sign of readiness. If possible, pass on the ground — although sometimes the second (return) pass is made in the air over an intervening defender. Make the second pass to the space where your teammate is running. The pass should be soft so the ball won't roll too far. If the space is small, the play is much more difficult and requires a faster pass to the feet. When working with a small space, plan what your next action will be. There is little time after receiving the ball.

Whether the wall pass is "on" or "off" is a judgement the wall player must make in a fraction of a second. The wall pass is "on" when the defender is beaten and it is safe to make a return pass. If the defender isn't beaten or the path for the return pass is obstructed, then the return pass is "off".

The wall pass is not only an important tool for beating defenders, but a psychological tool as well. Being beaten by soccer's oldest play is humiliating. The ability to do wall passes signifies a high level of technical and tactical sophistication. In addition, the wall pass is the foundation for more sophisticated three player combinations.

Figure 47 The Wall Pass

The requirements for a wall pass are a beatable defender with space behind them and an aware teammate in the proper position. The player with the ball passes to the feet of the second player and sprints around the defender for a return pass.

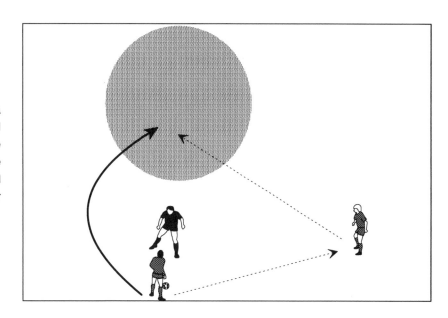

Switching Plays

Crossing movements characterize switching plays. A player to the right of the ball before the movement began will end up to the left of the ball or vice versa. Exchanging the ball during the movement creates a "takeover" (Fig. 48, pg. 44). The crossing movement can be preceded by a square pass — a "pass and follow" combination (Fig. 39, pg. 32).

Most combination plays are designed to beat defenders, but not switching plays. They keep possession, confuse or reshuffle the defense and exploit space that exists in a square position. However, defenders sometimes are beaten in the process.

The context in which these plays occur reflects their varied functions. They occur when a covered square player sees space on the other side of the ball and runs into it (Fig. 54, pg. 47); when the player with the ball moves toward a square player (Fig. 45, pg. 39); when a player is trapped with the ball in the corner or near the sidelines; or after a square pass, when the passer follows the pass and runs into a space (Fig. 59, pg. 49).

These switching movements have many advantages. They are "onside" movements with no risk of running into an offsides position. For that reason, they are especially useful when playing against the last line of defenders. Running behind the ball also keeps the runner in good defensive position if the ball is lost. Switching movements are confusing for the defense because they cross defensive lanes of coverage, creating uncertainty. Despite these many advantages teams under-utilize these creative movements. — probably because the movements are so disruptive when a team uses a rigid formation.

Figure 48 Switching and Takeovers

If the player with the ball dribbles toward a teammate, that teammate should move toward and behind them, switching or doing a takeover. Do not run away!

Through Pass to Space

The player with the ball passes to a player running into a space closer to goal. This is one of the simplest combination plays (Fig. 57, pg. 48).

Three Player Combinations

In a three player combination the basic play is a pass made to a player running into space. However, there is additional complexity as three players may work together to create the space and to disguise the run. In addition, new passing

Figure 49 Good Run?

No. This run is bad for two reasons. First, it is moving the second defender into a better defensive position close to goal. Second, the defender is not beatable (playing too loosely) so the run is a waste. The attacker would have been better off simply staying wide and square or waiting until his teammate was closer to goal, then running behind and around him. This would create defensive confusion and an improved scoring opportunity.

Figure 50 Good Run?

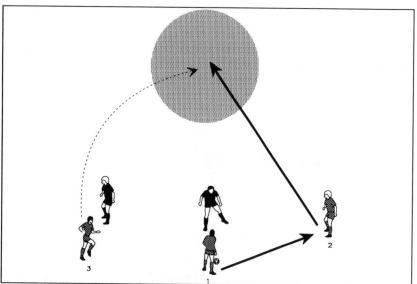

Figure 51 Three Player Combinations

Three player combinations, like wall passes, need a beatable defender with space behind them. However, a third player takes part. There are several variations. In this variation on a wall pass, the run to space is made by the third player.

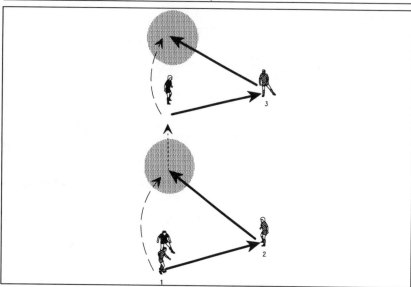

Figure 52 Three Player Combinations

This three player combination is simply two successive wall passes. The third player assists by setting the second wall.

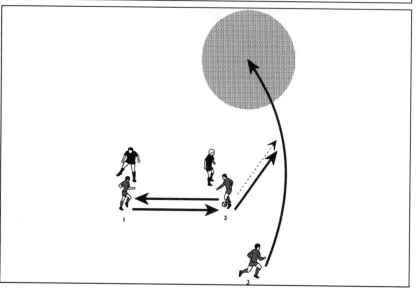

Figure 53 Three Player Combinations

In this three player combination two players do a takeover while a third runs into space for a pass. The crossfield dribble that starts the play creates the space necessary for the successful overlapping run. The initial crossfield movement also diverts attention away from the third player's run.

options are available. A player must therefore be aware of what space is accessible to their teammates and how to use them to get the ball to the player running into space. Attention can be diverted away from the player running into space by passing (Fig. 51, pg. 46), by player movement (Fig. 53, pg. 46) or both.

Recognition of a simple principle — get the ball to a player running into space — makes teamwork such as the three player combination possible. Although one player may not be able to pass directly to a space, they know a teammate can see the same opportunity and can complete the pass. Combination play is simple teamwork at its finest. It is one of the most creative, and enjoyable aspects of soccer. In each case the play depends on players recognizing a space and sharing a common conception of how to use that space.

2 vs. 2

"He who understands how to use both large and small forces will be victorious." Sun Tzu

Two players form the simplest team, and therefore the 2-on-2 conflict is a useful one to study. Tactical considerations of larger-sided conflicts apply, but are greatly simplified. Also, the 2-on-2 is a frequent subconflict in games with more than 2 players on a team. The 2-on-2 is unique in that the players must continually change roles — support, penetrate and create new opportunities as the situation demands. For this reason, the 2-on-2 provides a method for isolating and evaluating an individual's understanding of these concepts.

Figure 54 Boring and Basic

The player without the ball in a 2-on-2 spends most of their time running behind their teammate, from one square position to another. This is a good position for support and it helps prevent breakaways. It also tends to draw the second defender out of position, creating dribbling opportunities and rare chances for through passes behind the defense.

Figure 55 Penetrate by Dribbling

Sometimes the second attacker can draw the second (covering) defender out of a goal-side position. The player with the ball then has only one defender to beat and should dribble if they have the skill.

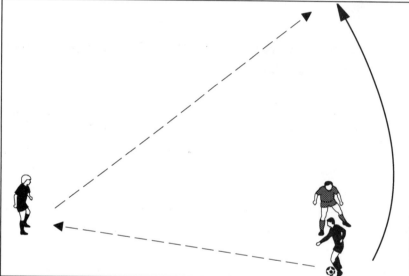

Figure 56 Wall Pass

When the defender at the ball is slow, inattentive or too close, the opportunity exists for a successful wall pass. The second attacker must be vigilant and move quickly to a position from which a successful return pass can be made. Any sudden sprint toward a space should stimulate one's passing reflex.

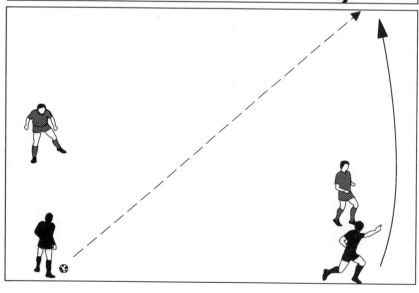

Figure 57 Penetrating Runs, 2-on-2
The second attacker spends most of their time behind or even with the ball. However, you can make penetrating runs when:

- You are covered tightly.
- There is space behind the marking defender.
- The player with the ball can easily pass to this space.
- The player with the ball has their head up and sees the opportunity.

Your sudden surge toward the space should trigger the pass.

Figure 58 Switching and Takeovers

Because most of the second player's runs are behind the ball, this creates frequent opportunities for takeovers and switching plays. These may confuse the defense and temporarily create an open player. A sprint to goal performed immediately after a takeover sometimes is effective in exploiting the confusion. It is also very effective on fastbreaks.

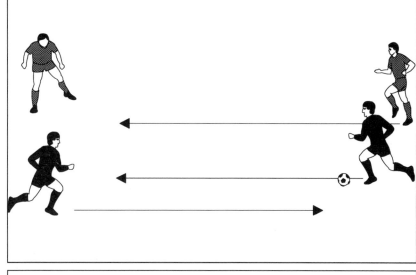

Figure 59 Pass and Overlap

Moving after passing is important. In 2-on-2 the most frequent movement is to follow the pass and run behind the pass recipient. This is a conservative run that keeps the player in a good defensive position if the pass is intercepted. The opportunity to confuse the defense with takeovers is created.

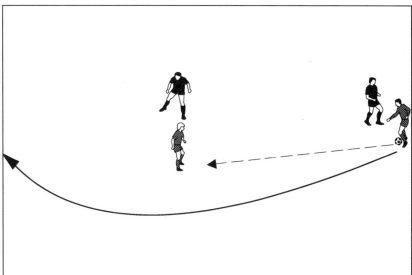

Figure 60 Pass and Run Through

Pass and sprint behind the defense when the defender is beatable and there is space behind the defense. This is how wall passes start. If you don't get the ball circle around and come back square on the other side. Running through after passing is more common when you have confidence in your teammate's ability to protect the ball. If your teammate is weak, limit your runs to through space—pass and overlap instead.

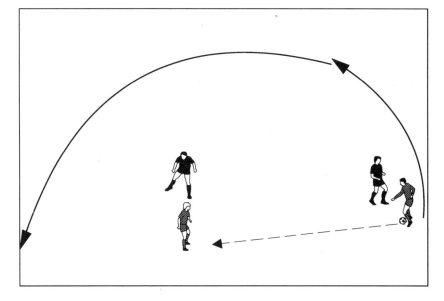

Possession

To keep the ball in the 2-on-2, the teammate of the person with the ball must know when and how to support. Support when your teammate is in trouble (often suggested by a head down position), such as when there is great defensive pressure. Support by moving to a space where the ball can be passed. This is usually to one side and behind the person —a square position (Fig. 27, pg. 26).

The player without the ball will spend most of their time crossing behind the person with the ball — from one square position to the other (Fig. 54, pg. 47). There are two reasons for this — the sudden need for support, and preventing breakaways. In larger-sided conflicts, additional players can provide support and defensive safety, allowing greater freedom of movement.

Penetration

In the 2-on-2, dribbling, passing and combination plays create penetration. If the player with the ball is a good dribbler, the second player can attempt to help by dragging away any covering defender (Fig. 55, pg. 48) or by confusing the defense temporarily with runs behind the ball (Fig. 54, pg. 47).

Possible combination plays include the wall pass, through passes to space, and takeovers. A tightly covering defender (beatable) creates the opportunity for a through pass (Fig. 57, pg. 48). This is one of the few times the player without the ball should run toward goal. The opportunity for the wall pass arises when there is space behind a beatable defender marking at the ball (Fig. 56, pg. 48). Takeovers occur whenever the player with the ball dribbles toward the square player or the square player runs behind the player with the ball (Fig. 58, pg. 49).

Creating New Opportunities

Beatable defenders with space behind them create the best chances to penetrate the defense. When there are no opportunities for penetration, the offense tries to create new possibilities by taking on the defense or by moving. If you have the skill, shake things up by trying to beat a defender. Even if you don't get past the defender, you

Vision

Simple things make a difference. In soccer, two of the most important elements of a successful offense require neither skill nor tactical sophistication — staying spread out and having good vision. There is nothing as simple, yet more important to the success of a soccer team, than good vision. By vision we mean the personal habit of constantly scrutinizing the soccer field to get the big picture. Soccer players should look over the entire field approximately every five seconds. They should note the best place for the ball (usually an area of space) and the location of nearby passing opportunities. On defense, players should check the space behind them and plan what to do when they get the ball.

Players with vision are distinguished by their apparent ability to perceive events before they happen, and by their ability to influence play by appropriately redistributing the ball. Players with vision are a prerequisite for implementing a system of total football.

How do we develop players with vision? First, develop skill. A player that is a slave to the ball can't be looking around the field. The habit of looking before the ball is received can be encouraged by scrimmaging with a one-touch restriction. Games with multiple goals also reward players with vision. Another technique is making a loud noise (beating a gong, blowing a special whistle) every five seconds to remind players how often to look around. In reviewing a videotape of a game, it is easy to point out the times when a player with good vision could have capitalized on a particular situation. Players should become very familiar with the phrase "Don't be a ball-watcher!"

may draw the other defender, leaving your teammate open for a pass. Passing square and then running behind (overlapping) the pass recipient, may loosen things up (Fig. 59, pg. 49). Running through after a square pass is less common because there are graver consequences if the pass is intercepted (Fig. 60, pg. 49).

5 vs. 5

The five-on-five conflict is useful to study because it has all the close passing options — through, right, left and back. It is also a common size for indoor teams. The basic movements in this conflict involve producing right, left, through, and back passing options. Instead of a back player, a team may decide to keep the two square players deep, freeing an additional through player.

Possession

Possession is easy to maintain if the team always provides deep square players to the right and left of the ball. Unfortunately, one situation where teams are lax about providing both these options is when the ball is near the sidelines. A player from the middle should make a run downline (Fig. 26, pg. 25). This movement not only provides support and another passing option, but also creates space in the middle of the field.

Square players must move when closely covered (Fig. 29, pg. 26). Commonly, they will sprint to goal, and one of the through players will come back to fill the space they create. Sometimes a covered player can get open by making a run behind the ball (Fig. 54, pg. 47). With tight individual markings these measures may not work. Fortunately, tight markings create opportunities for beating defenders by runs to space (Fig. 57, pg. 48), wall passes and other combination plays.

Penetration

The means of penetration used in the 2-on-2 (dribbling, wall pass, penetrating run) are still applicable in the 5-on-5. The presence of through players creates new opportunities, particularly, three player combinations. Not only is the through pass to a player's feet an option, but three player combinations using that as the initial pass are possible. The through pass is followed by a return ball played to players sprinting forward into space or the sides or back of the through player (Fig. 38, pg. 32). The simple addition of one player greatly multiplies the offensive options.

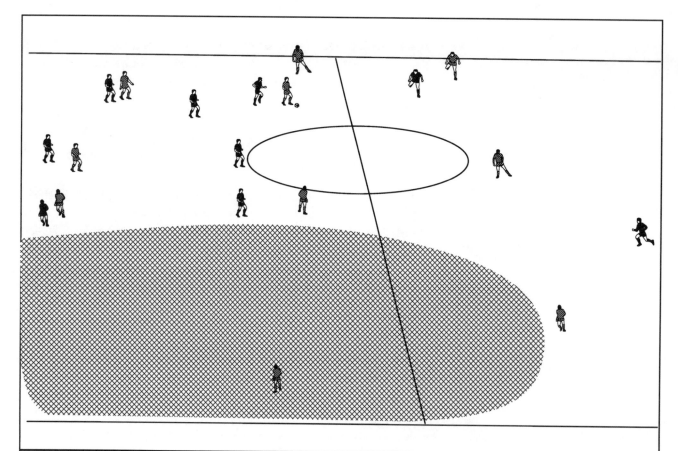

Figure 61 Get the Big Picture

It is surprising how few players would recognize this large space (cross-hatched). During the excitement of the game, with all the immediate pressure, only the best players are able to grasp the big picture. Average players only see the two or three players in the immediate vicinity. They often pass to the first player that has the same jersey color. The attack gets mired down in a bunch and possession is lost. To be a truly great team requires eleven players with good vision; eleven players that work together to create large useful spaces; and eleven players that can work together to move the ball swiftly to those spaces. Are you short-sighted or do you see the big picture?

Creating New Opportunities

As in the 2-on-2, the principle methods are dribbling and "pass and move" combinations. With another square player and a back player, through runs are less risky and more frequent than in 2-on-2.

11 vs. 11

An 11-sided game has all the elements of the smaller-sided competitions plus players away from the ball. The biggest difficulties are organizing all these players, keeping them spread out, and keeping them from duplicating each

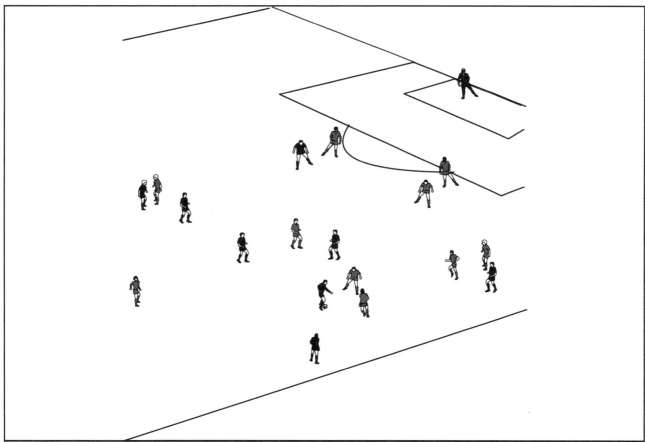

Figure 62 Amateurs Bunch, Professionals Don't!

Bunches are created from the grandest, most unselfish emotion — the desire to help a friend in trouble. Unfortunately, like the application of leeches in ancient medicine, these good intentions only make things worse. The player with the ball needs only right, left, through and back passing options. Moving more players to the ball just draws more defenders, making less useful space, smaller passing lanes and a more efficient and aggressive defense. If the players around the ball cannot get open they should sprint away, creating space — then they can be re-placed. Piling more people around the ball does not help — it makes things worse!

Not only are there too many players in a bunch, but frequently they are far too close together. Keep a minimum of 10 yards whenever possible. More space is better. It draws players away from the ball, opens up passing lanes, gives everyone more time, and isolates defenders making them less efficient. Show some intelligence — spread out!

other's efforts. It is easy to understand why formations arose. To play without formations, one must carefully build up from the smaller-sided games, continually emphasizing staying spread out, having good field vision, and the importance of players away from the ball (Table 9). Because this is so difficult, particularly for young and unskilled players, it is yet another reason for using small-sided games with these groups. The players away from the ball are what distinguish this size conflict from the smaller-sided games.

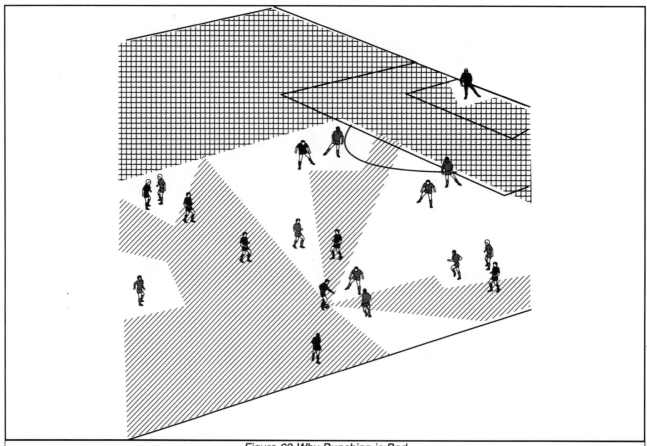

Figure 63 Why Bunching is Bad

Bunching creates tremendous spaces (double cross-hatch). This is good, no? It is true that to create large spaces players must concentrate, as around a bunch; but, it becomes virtually impossible to pass to the large spaces that are created. The passing lanes are extremely narrow (single cross-hatch) and the attack is doomed. Also, the spaces are useless because teammates are in the bunch, not in the spaces. When bunching to create space, do it in front of, and slightly away from the ball so passing lanes to the space are open (See Fig. 14, pg. 11).

Possession

The basis of possession is similar to 5-on-5. In 11-on-11 there are more players to fill any open positions around the ball. This results in more creative play and better opportunities, particularly when players behind the ball move to fill open passing options. Additional support can be provided by players farther from the ball.

With 11-on-a-side, attackers and defenders often bunch around the ball (Fig. 63, pg. 54). This makes maintaining possession extremely difficult. Prevent bunching (Table 10) by maintaining discipline so that more players don't move to the ball, teaching good field vision, and not playing the ball too long in one area. If the opponent is aggressive, only three passes can be made in an

Functions of Players Away From the Ball

- Draw defensive players away from ball
- Divert defensive attention away from ball
- Create passing options
- Create spaces for teammates

Table 9.

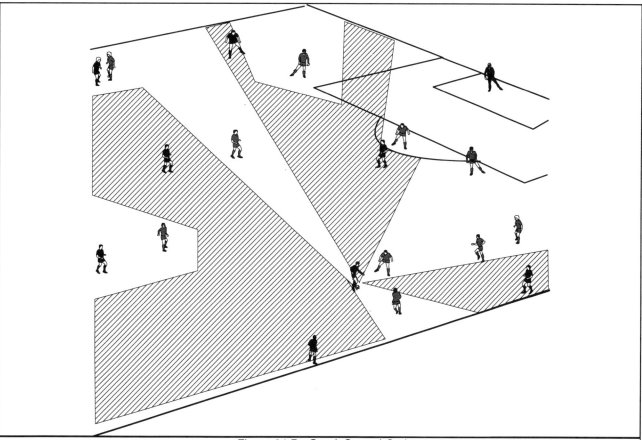

Figure 64 Be Good, Spread Out!

The players from the previous figure have been spread out. At first glance, the changes aren't too impressive. The huge spaces away from the ball have been broken up. It would still be difficult to make a successful long pass — because the players are covered. However, now the passing lane to the center goal area is significantly larger. A pass can be made to the player positioned near the top of the "D." This player has some space to maneuver as well as other good options. There is also room for some combination play or the player with the ball could dribble to goal with a reasonable chance of success. Spreading out is a small thing, but it is the sum of many small things that makes a great team.

area before it becomes crowded. With an aggressive opponent, dribbling produces a crowd even faster. Dribbling should be restricted to uncrowded areas or to crossfield movements. With good field vision, players can recognize the crowded mess around the ball and see where the ball should be. Hopefully, they will then switch the point of attack to a less crowded area.

With eleven players, the attacking team must be able to quickly switch the field of play to take advantage of space (Fig. 65, pg. 56). Continually switching the attack and using back passes helps spread out the defense (gives the attack "width and depth"). Bunches are less likely to form and the attack will have a greater chance of success.

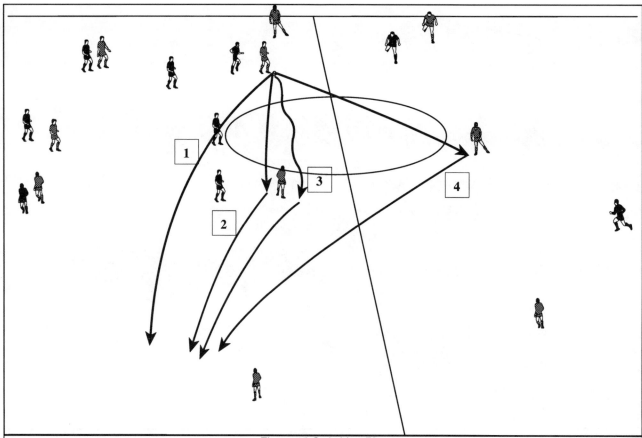

Figure 65 Switching Play

Being successful with eleven players not only requires the ability to create and see large spaces, but the ability to quickly move the ball to those spaces. This is called "switching the field of play". This figure depicts four methods.

1. A single long pass
2. Two shorter passes
3. Crossfield run with a pass
4. Back pass then cross

Of these four methods, the single long pass is the fastest, but will only be successful when there are huge spaces such as this (unusual). All of the other methods require more time. The space is often gone or has reappeared on the other side by the time the ball has been switched. This process of switching the attack and pursuing space is continual. It is part of the patient process of building the attack.

Penetration

All the methods of penetration applicable to 5-on-5 apply to 11-on-11, but, because of the additional players, there are more passing options. The problem isn't so much getting players to create these options, as getting them to see these options, and to work as a team to use them.

Preventing Bunches
• Stay spread out
• Only 3 players near the ball
• Only 3 passes in an area
• Change field frequently
• Limit dribbling
• Get the Big Picture

Table 10.

Creating New Opportunities

The methods of creating new opportunities are the same as 5-on-5, but enriched by the possibilities of changing the field of play and stretching out the defense. The back pass begins to play a more important role in the process. As in other aspects of full-sized teams, good field vision (See Box Text pg. 50) by all players is a requirement.

Figure 66 Photo by Phil Stephens

58

Chapter 3

The Individual Attacker

"All warfare is based on deception" Sun Tzu

Summary: What do I do when I have the ball? Do I dribble? Do I pass? In which direction? To whom? The answers to these and many other questions will decide the outcome of a soccer game. Because it is fastest, passing is the preferred means of getting the ball to different points on the field. We dribble when there are no good passing options, when necessary to keep possession and when there is only one defender to beat for a shot. Weigh the benefits of an action (e.g., completing a pass, beating a defender) against the consequences of failure (losing the ball).

We classify the defenders we meet in one-on-ones as either passive and aggressive. In both cases we beat the defender by playing the ball past them and beating them to it — tasks that are more difficult than they sound. Beating defenders requires ball control, deception, timing and knowledge.

Decisions, Options and Risk

A single game of soccer involves thousands of decisions — decisions that determine the game's outcome. Typical examples include: Do I keep the ball or pass? Where should I pass? For the individual, making a decision means weighing the various options available. The number of options available will depend on the skill of the player and the ability of the player's teammates to create more options.

The likelihood of a soccer action (passing, beating a defender) "working" depends on the difficulty of the task and the options available. Skilled players have more options and therefore have a better chance of success. The skilled player can consider dribbling out of situations impossible for others, can complete passes others wouldn't attempt and can make shots others couldn't imagine. Although the decision-making process becomes complex with the player's expanded options, the probability of success becomes greater.

There are few decisions that aren't the result of weighing the potential benefits and consequences of a given action — risk. A team takes few risks in the area around its own goal, because failure (losing the ball) has serious consequences (opponent scores). This concern with safety in the defensive end severely limits a player's options, often making play difficult in this area. As attacking players proceed from the defensive end to the offensive end of the field they take more chances and have more options. The necessity of scoring goals means that players must attempt actions that have little chance of success. Scorers must become risk takers and dare to do the improbable or unpredictable. Players will not score goals unless they learn to seize small opportunities, to accept the responsibility of making an attempt (it is easier to pass to someone else) — to shoot, shoot, shoot! The consequences of failure have become fewer in the attacking end, while the benefits of success have become greater.

Advanced Planning

In the moments when you don't have the ball, you must prepare for the time when you will. What would you do if the ball arrived unexpectedly? You should have a safety outlet in mind — an open teammate for emergency passes. Continually update your plans with the changing field situation.

Check the entire field every three to five seconds, or with every movement of the ball. You should know where the greatest opportunities on the field are — areas where players have the most space. When the ball arrives, you'll be ready to do your part to move the ball to where it can do the most good.

Now You've Got the Ball

When receiving a pass, it is important to move to the ball, particularly if there are defenders nearby or if you don't know where the nearest opponents are. If you have been looking and planning, you'll know whether you need to take immediate action,because of an opportunity (to make a pass or to shoot) or a threat (defender approaching fast).

The first and most important decision is whether to continue playing the ball in the immediate area or to switch the field of play. If there is useful local space, search first for opportunities to make through passes. If none exist, look for beatable defenders that may be marking you or covering other players. Beatable defenders create opportunities for you to dribble, start a wall pass or (if someone else is being marked by a beatable defender) complete other passes. If these opportunities are not available, you must try to create new opportunities by challenging a defender, by passing and moving, or by changing the field of play.

"Appear at places to which he must hasten; move swiftly where he does not expect you." Sun Tzu.

You can change the field of play with a single, long crossing ball (often easily intercepted), by two shorter passes, by a cross-field run or by a back pass followed by a cross (Fig. 65, pg. 56). Continually monitoring the whole field will help you make far-sighted, sensible decisions that will benefit your team (Fig. 61, pg. 52).

Decisions About Passing

Players should pass the ball when they are in danger of losing possession or when there is a teammate available who could use it more effectively (Fig. 67, pg. 62). Pass to maintain possession, to penetrate the defense and to create new opportunities. If in doubt, the safe rule is this: "Pass to the player with the most space". This rule applies whether the player is ahead of you, alongside you or behind you, and it especially applies when you are in trouble.

To know which place is best for the ball, develop good field vision (see Vision page 50). Passing options must be created and they must be seen. Generally, the ball belongs in the area with the fewest defenders — where the attack is most likely to be successful. Also consider the skill of the pass recipient and their options — players in the middle of the field generally have more options.

Figure 67 Dribble or Pass?

Generally, we pass when we can safely get the ball to someone in a better attacking position than our-selves. In this case, the player upfield is in better position, being closer to goal, with equal space.

Figure 68 Passing Functions

Passes are made to keep possession, to advance the ball, switch the attack, to score and to create space. This se-quence illustrates how a pass creates space. This through pass was not kept, but immediately passed back. Never-theless, it drew nearby defenders, cre-ating more space square and back. This is an important tactic in building the attack.

Figure 69 Passing Functions

What is a Good Pass?

A good pass is accurate, has the correct speed (pace) and is well-timed. Few can appreciate the accuracy that is obtainable by a skilled player. The skilled player can deftly thread the ball between two moving defenders (sometimes through their legs) and hit the right foot of the intended recipient. This degree of accuracy, when it is common on a team, tremendously increases the ability to penetrate the defense. It also allows the team to play at a much faster tempo because players don't have to stop or move backwards for a ball, or control it before shooting.

Accuracy alone is not sufficient. The pass must be moving at the right speed (have the right pace). If the ball is moving too fast it will be hard to control, go out of bounds or go to an opponent. If the pass is too slow it will be intercepted or the player will have to wait or move toward it, slowing the game. When you receive a pass from the best players you may not even have to control it — it will be waiting neatly in your path for you to collect, or be moving nicely along with you.

The last measure of a good pass is timing. The pass must be released at the right time — to thread the needle, or to keep you from being offsides.

Although many players consider themselves excellent passers, few really have the accuracy, pace and timing to be called a "master passer". Do you?

Through Pass — Penetrating the Defense

Through passes feel good because they advance the ball; they penetrate the defense and take the ball closer to goal. The same directness that makes through passes the most desirable also makes them the most difficult to execute, because the defense places a priority on preventing them. A player must often be beaten for the pass to be made, and the receiving player is often covered. Through passes also can create space as defenders cluster around the receiving player, abandoning areas that they were guarding (Fig. 68 & 69, pg. 62). Because of this, through passes are often useful in starting combination plays. Players sprint into the spaces created by the through pass and receive the ball. If it can be safely completed, a penetrating pass is always a player's first choice.

Square Pass — Keeping Possession

The most common pass, the square pass, neither advances nor retreats; it is played across the field or perpendicular to the path to goal. Often teammates to the side of, or "square", are open and visible to a pressured player. Square passes to these players are essential for maintaining possession. Long square passes spread defenders out across the width of the field, making penetration easier. Use square passes to switch the point of attack to an area where it may be more successful.

Each player on the field has a unique perspective, and unique passing angles. Better players become conscious of the passing angles of their teammates and use teammates to complete passes that they cannot. In this way, square passes often precede through passes in combination plays designed to penetrate the defense — e.g., wall passes. Remember square passes for keeping possession, giving width to the attack (stretching the defense wide), changing the point of attack and for finding players that can complete through passes.

Back Pass — Necessary and Under-Utilized

Many players misunderstand and under-utilize back passes. Although they may seem like steps backward, back passes are valuable. Teammates in the back position are more likely than all others to be open. They have the best view of the field, can best determine where the ball should be, and can often successfully redistribute the ball (Fig. 70, pg. 64). Back passes create space forward when the defense moves to pressure the pass recipient. So, a back pass often becomes a prelude to a pass that changes the field of play or penetrates the defense. Back passes are also handy for consuming time when a team has a lead. When attacking, a back pass from the goal area often finds an open player with a better scoring angle.

Make a long back pass to retain possession when pressured and to secure possession when unexpectedly receiving the ball from an opponent. Don't make the common mistake of returning such a gift by trying to force play forward in the same area. A long back pass secures possession and gets the ball to a player who has more time and a much better view of the field. As a soccer team improves the number of back passes increases.

Figure 70 Back Pass

The player with the ball has two passing alternatives, a back pass to the goalie or a long square pass. Which is best? In this case, the best pass is a back pass. The square pass is likely to be intercepted and the defender is positioned with that in mind. As is frequently the case, the recipient of the back pass has lots of time, has good passing angles, and a good view of the field. On average, one-third of passes should be back passes. (Note: The square player should back up a little.)

Figure 71 Pass to Space or to Feet?
When a player has space pass to their feet. If a player is tightly marked and there is space behind the defender, pass to that space. You must take into consideration the player's speed and skill. If you want the ball played to your feet, face the ball. If you want the ball played to a space, face the space. For a successful pass to space, both players must work together to coordinate their activities. The run to space must occur only when it is seen. The sudden acceleration toward the space triggers the pass.

To Space or to Feet?

Players are often uncertain about whether to pass to a teammate's feet or to the space behind the marking defender (Fig. 71, pg. 64). The answer depends on how tightly the covering player is marking, and on the speed and ability of the individual receiving player. If the receiving player has space, then it is safer to pass to their feet. When closely covered, the preferred pass is to the space behind the defender. A fast teammate often prefers passes to space, while slower or trickier teammates prefer passes to their feet.

Players can use body language to show where they want the ball. Often, receiving players face the space if they want the ball sent in that direction. If they want the ball played to their feet, they face the passer.

Push Passes — A Note on Technique

The most important passing technique is the inside-the-foot pass, or push pass. Approximately 70 percent of passes in a professional game are of this type. Unfortunately, amateurs use this pass much less frequently. The virtue of the pass is its great accuracy — essential at the game's highest levels. No player can be *too* good at this pass (Fig. 72, pg. 65 & Fig. 200, pg. 186).

Figure 72 Passing Technique

You have to master the "inside-of-the-foot pass" or "push" pass. It is the most important pass in soccer because of its accuracy. The body faces the target with legs slightly bent. The planted foot points to the target. The kicking toe is up and the foot rigid. The striking surface is the back-half of the foot, toward the heel. The ball is struck in the middle. The kicking leg moves in a straight line toward the target until the ball leaves the foot. In the follow-through the kicking leg will rotate, come up and bend. The final position will be with the kicking leg bent 90 degrees, with both the knee cap and toe pointing at the target. The follow-through is important for power and accuracy. Also see page 186.

The Importance of Dribbling

Any given game of soccer encompasses many smaller conflicts involving varying numbers of people. For example, a small group of three or four attackers and as many defenders often surround the ball. At the center of this crowd, at the ball, is a one-on-one conflict. The team that dominates in the series of one-on-one conflicts usually wins the game. This is no coincidence, winning one-on-ones is the most important means of creating space. Beating a defender by dribbling puts the attacker in space behind the defender and creates space away from the ball by drawing other defenders to the ball (Fig. 21, pg. 14). A team dominant in one-on-ones continually compromises the opponent's defense. It advances the ball without difficulty and its scoring opportunities multiply. If a team is dominant in one-on-ones, its offense will take care of itself. It is only when both teams have roughly equal one-on-one skills that other offensive tactics become significant.

There are many unfortunate consequences of being weaker in one-on-ones. A team with little dribbling skill tends to bunch — to help the player with the ball and out of fear of a turnover. Attacking players become reluctant to make runs because they must be available nearby for a pass or to defend if the ball is lost. Defenders become more confident and aggressive. Defensive markings away from the ball become tighter as there is less need to back up the defender at the ball. The net result is an intimidated offense that will have trouble advancing the ball by any means — dribbling or passing.

When to Dribble

Because it's quicker, passing is the preferred way of getting the ball from point A to point B. Dribbling (carrying the ball with the feet) is often necessary when passing is too risky or impossible. A skilled dribbler can often penetrate a crowd of defend-

When to Dribble at Goal
• To advance the ball across open space
• To go for a shot
• To beat one defender
• To create new opportunities

Table 11

When to Dribble Back
• To maintain possession
• To draw out defense

Table 12

Figure 73 How Long to Keep the Ball

It is safe to keep the ball as long as you have space. Sometimes when you have space you will pass anyway just to get the ball to a better offensive position or to keep it moving. When you are facing your own keeper and receive a ball (as in this picture), you should generally play the ball back without stopping it (one-touch). To attempt to turn is extremely risky and should be done only if you know you are clear, when told by teammates that you are clear, or when going for a shot on goal. Sometimes you will be able to make a square pass to teammates running up from behind.

Figure 74 The Power of Dribbling

Where to Dribble

Beating defenders by dribbling is the most important, most direct means of creating space. When you go around a defender another defender must move to cover you. This rearrangement of defensive coverage usually creates defensive confusion and one or more open attackers — good passing targets. In most cases, the team with the best one-on-one skills will win a match.

ers more effectively than players attempting close passing. Here are some guidelines for deciding when to dribble: Dribble (challenge the defender) when one defender is between you and goal, to keep possession (no passing options), to confuse the defense and to create new offensive opportunities. Dribble to advance the ball across large open spaces if a pass isn't available.

When to Dribble Crossfield
• No space forward
• When defender cannot be beaten one-on one
• For easier shot on goal
• To change field of play
• To confuse defenders
• When necessary to keep possession

Table 13

Once you know that it's appropriate to dribble, in which direction should you go? The inexperienced player generally goes right to goal, but this is not always best. If you are at an offensive advantage (for example, a two-on-one), head for goal. If you have an open field with no downfield passing options, or if you have just one defender to beat for a shot on goal, then going to goal also makes sense (Table 11).

Soccer is not usually a straight-ahead game. It requires intelligence and creativity. Players that only go straight ahead are similar to dogs who think that the only way to the bone on the other side of the fence is to go through the fence, jump it or dig under it. Sometimes you have to back up and go around.

Dribbling across the field is a creative and under-used option (Table 13). It is very difficult for defenders to stop and often creates defensive confusion. Players should dribble across the field when there is no space toward goal, when the defender cannot be beaten one-on-one, when maneuvering for an easier shot, when it is advisable to change the field of play, when seeking to confuse the defense (creating new opportunities), and when necessary to keep possession. Cross-field dribbling is creative and productive.

A player commonly dribbles in the direction of their goal (back) to avoid pressure and keep possession (Table 12). This is appropriate when a player needs to find space and open teammates. Dribbling back is also a tactic to draw opponents from defensive positions, creating space closer to goal. The ball must be dribbled (or passed) back to switch play from a bunch.

When Not to Dribble

Part of knowing when to dribble is knowing when not to dribble. Too often the first impulse of a player upon receiving the ball is to plow as far downfield as possible without looking up. It is generally better to stop the ball, look over the field and make an appropriate pass. Preserving space in this way gains players time — time to decide on the best course of action, time for teammates to create passing options and time to prepare for any oncoming threat. Simply stopping and getting your head up sends an important signal to your opponents that you are a good player. A "heads-up" player (Fig. 75, pg. 68) usually has a skill level that allows them to control the ball without watching it. Heads-up players are busy looking over the whole field for opportunities rather than watching the ball. Also, because players usually get their head up prior to passing, opponents become more concerned with covering for passes than preventing the dribbling threat. For these reasons players with their heads up are less likely to be pressured. Pressure is also less likely to be effective because a heads-up player can see and avoid any threats. Play like a smart player, keep your head up.

Uses of Fakes
• To beat defenders
• To back off aggressive defenders
• To create defensive confusion
• To create new opportunities
• To disguise one's intentions
• To demonstrate superiority

Table 14

Advantages of Going Slowly
Dribbling is easier when moving slowly. The ball is easier to control, passes are more accurate, and you can see better. Because your acceleration is greatest when going slowly, it is often easier to beat defenders. Experienced players reserve fast speeds for when there is a temporary advantage, such as a breakaway.

Figure 75 Heads-Up Player

"Heads-Up" is a literal description that has become a figure of speech. Good players keep their heads-up. This allows them to see opportunities over the field. They can also see danger and plan accordingly. The heads-up players are the playmakers. Becoming a heads-up player requires mastering ball skills so you don't have to look at the ball. It also requires vision, knowledge of the game, and knowledge of one's teammates.

Figure 76 Step-over Fake

Figure 76 Step-over Fake

Fakes

"Be as coy as a hare and as swift as the fox and you are invincible. "
Sun Tzu

Making a running step over the ball is an effective fake. Depending on the context and how the motion is performed it may simulate a pass, shot, false start, or change of direction. In this photo the action is a false start. This motion may move the defender enough to allow the attacker to cut and go to the middle of the field or pass to the center area. The fake will probably make the defender more cautious — the attacker will be given a little more space. Fakes are an important tool against aggressive defenders.

Fakes (feints) distinguish players with advanced skill. These players know that anything in soccer (traps, changes of direction, shots, stops, starts, passes) can be faked, that is — imitated or abbreviated. If done properly, the person executing the fake will have the option of either doing the fake or completing the motion and doing the real thing. The opponent's response during the fake's execution dictates the option chosen.

Figure 77 Fakes

Some fakes are easier to do when moving fast. This head and body fake is created by simply twisting and dipping away from the intended direction. Because the legs are not involved, control is less likely to be lost.

Fakes have many uses (Table 14). Use fakes to move defenders and to create uncertainty. False starts (Fig. 195, pg. 182), false changes of direction (Fig. 77, pg. 69) and shooting (Fig. 198, pg. 184) fakes move defenders or put them off balance. Before the defender can stop and change direction the attacker can be heading the other way or going past (Fig. 85, pg. 75).

Fakes should be appropriate for the situation. If a defender is too close, do a false start. If the options are to dribble left or right, fake left then go right. If the defense is expecting a pass, fake a pass then dribble. With practice fakes will become automatic and appropriate.

Fakes can disguise one's intentions. Predictable attackers are easily defended. If an attacker really changes direction every time they appear to be about to change direction, the defender can soon anticipate and intercept the ball. If, on the other hand, an attacker mixes fake changes of direction with the real thing, the defender can't anticipate. In the same way, it is important to create confusion about whether a pass is to be made and its direction. An attacker with excellent fakes can cause an entire defense to shift with a good faked pass. This can be a very powerful tool in creating new opportunities. Fakes create defensive movement and uncertainty, improving the chances of offensive success.

Fakes also can create space. When the player with the ball does fakes the covering defender becomes uncertain about their intentions. To gain time to evaluate the situation the defender gives the attacker more space.

Fakes become especially important and effective when the player with the ball is being heavily pressured — unfortunately, this is the most difficult time to

Figure 78 Face-Off

Facing the defender offers the greatest offensive possibilities but at the same time the ball is the most vulnerable. The offensive advantages are vision of the space toward goal and the options of moving or passing right, left or toward goal. This is the only stance if you are going to beat your covering defender by dribbling. This is a weak defensive stance because the ball is exposed, unshielded by your body.

think of them. With a few fakes the defender will usually stop pressuring and stay a more comfortable distance away. If the defender doesn't retreat, fakes will usually cause such a serious misstep that the attacker can beat the defender. When next facing the same defender, the attacker will be given more room. Fakes are an important means of neutralizing aggressive, pressuring defenders and should be a normal part of a player's dribbling style.

One-on-One Stance

During dribbling an attacker's body position in relation to an opponent shouldn't be accidental. The attacker must decide whether to face the defender, be half-turned or be completely turned away. Each of these positions has advantages and disadvantages. The attacker's chosen stance depends on their position when receiving the ball, the need to protect the ball, the direction of intended movement, skill, speed, and their plans.

Facing Defenders

Facing marking defenders offers you the highest visibility and the most options (Fig. 78, pg. 70). In this stance, you can see the space behind the defense and the opportunity to make a penetrating pass. While facing the defender you can dribble, make through passes or square passes to the right or left. Because of the number of options, the defensive job is more difficult.

Most players who intend to beat their covering defender assume a position facing the defender. Positioned in this way, you can push the ball past, then

Figure 79 Facing Sideways

Facing sideways is a compromise position. The ball can be well screened but offensive possibilities are limited. Vision is restricted to one direction and it is difficult to play the ball toward goal. Creative lateral movements follow naturally from this position.

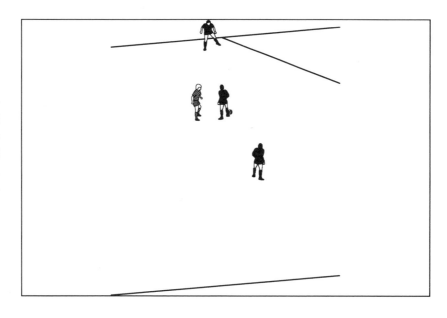

beat them to it. The basic steps of winning a one-on-one are easiest when you confront the defender face to face.

When pressured by two defenders, this is also the best stance (passing is always the best action). If you can't pass to a teammate, face the defenders, keep them both in sight, and attempt to go between them. This is better than attempting to screen the ball from them. Attacking often succeeds because of surprise and confusion.

The disadvantage of facing the defender is the vulnerability of the ball; facing exposes the ball to an opponent who is only three feet away. Only quick feet, fakes and the proper reflexes keep the defender from getting the ball. Until you develop these skills, you are vulnerable when the ball is unshielded.

Half-Turned

When half-turned, your shoulder is toward the defender (Fig. 79, pg. 71). This is a half-defensive, half-offensive posture with a good view of half the field. Square and through passing options exist, but only in the direction you are facing. From this stance it is easy to dribble cross-field, to do take-overs and to complete wall passes. It's probably the best position for protecting the ball from an aggressive defender — because the ball is kept at the maximum distance. It is hard to beat marking defenders from this stance because it's difficult to push the ball behind them. In summary, half-turned is a position that

Figure 80 Fully Turned

The completely turned attacker has only limited options and limited visibility. It is also very difficult to successfully turn with an opponent on one's back. For these reasons, it is better to avoid this stance by back passing when possible. Although protecting the ball from a half-turned stance is preferred, this attacker is doing a good job of demonstrating how to shield the ball and use the foot farthest from the defender for control.

Figure 81 Holding The Ball When Turned

In the middle and attacking thirds of the field, a player is more likely to screen a ball for a while when fully turned. This allows teammates the opportunity to support and make runs. Here, a teammate is about to make an overlapping run behind the ball. This is another good example of screening the ball.

Figure 82 Turned, Near Goal

When fully-turned near goal the preferred option is to turn and shoot. In this case the ball will probably be passed back because the angle is poor. Turning may be possible because the defender's extremely close position prevents the defender from seeing the ball — the defender reacts to body directional fakes. A defender that is too aggressive in coming around the attacker for the ball is beaten by pivoting (Fig. 98, pg. 84).

allows good protection of the ball while not totally removing offensive options.

Fully-Turned

When fully-turned, you are facing your goalkeeper with the opponent on your back (Fig. 80, pg. 72). Although a good means of protecting the ball, this position has several drawbacks. Vision is extremely restricted so it is difficult to see passing options. Turning is generally unsafe, because you can't see what trouble lurks. Attempt to turn only if the defender is five or more feet away or when the defender is touching. With the defender touching, directional fakes become effective as does simply screening the ball and pivoting around the defender. Dribbling back is a second option. If the defender doesn't follow, you can safely turn. If the defender follows aggressively you may be able to take advantage of their momentum by a sudden cut to the side. Dribbling and turning are poor choices in every part of the field except near the opponent's goal — first-time back passing is recommended. To be successful playing close to goal (Fig. 82, pg. 73) learn to turn and shoot or play the ball square or back from this position. After receiving the ball shield it, and wait for teammates to make runs forward (Fig. 81, pg. 73).

Figure 83 Speed

Dribbling can be seen as a two part task, getting the ball past the defender and then beating them to it. In this situation the one-on-one has been reduced to a simple foot race.

Figure 84 Changing Direction

There are many ways to change direction. Perhaps the two most common are by a chopping lateral cut and by reversing direction with the sole of the foot. Many good dribblers are successful just because of this skill. Notice, how the defender, in his quest for the ball, has moved in front of the dribbler. This not only makes a change of direction a winning move but a necessary one. Learning to change direction quickly in many ways will help you beat defenders. It is also a survival skill.

Introduction to Beating Defenders

Beating defenders requires two simple steps: pushing the ball past the defender and beating them to it (Fig. 87, pg. 76). This simplicity is deceptive for there are many complicating elements that make it more an art than a science. An important complication is the skill required. Without a high level of skill your concentration must be on the ball, not on the opponent you are trying to beat. Handling the ball must be an automatic, reflex-controlled activity. In most cases quick reflexes are not sufficient, you must learn the art of deception — fakes and false body language are essential for success. Knowledge plus these

Figure 85 Momentum

The momentum of a defender that approaches too rapidly will make them beatable. If the attacker can avoid the initial rush, the time it takes the defender to stop and change direction can be used to get away. Notice the attacker's use of a head and shoulder fake.

Figure 86 Momentum

skills create the confidence and poise necessary for evaluating dribbling situations and planning a response.

Your dribbling style will be dictated partly by your ability to accelerate. If you are very quick, you may want to use slow speeds to lull defenders, then surprise them with your acceleration. Although blinding speed is a tremendous advantage in beating defenders, the slow attacker isn't helpless. A slow attacker can beat defenders that approach too fast or position too closely (by pushing the ball between their legs or by using the wall pass). If you are slower, put the defender in motion before using fakes and changes of direction to create an advantage.

Space separates two players engaged in a one-on-one. This space acts as a buffer zone, providing each player with time to respond to the other. An important part of winning one-on-ones is knowing how and when to safely decrease or cross this space.

It takes time to change the momentum of a moving defender. Because of this, the faster a defender is moving, the greater their vulnerability to rapid changes of speed or direction by an attacking player. Any time the attacker and defender are moving in different directions or at different speeds, large exploitable momentum differences exist. Examples of such momentum differences include: an attacker standing still with an aggressive approaching defender, an attacker moving forward with a defender approaching from their side, and an attacker approaching a defender that is standing still. Skilled attackers not only recognize these situations but deliberately work to create conditions where momentum will work to their advantage. An attacker that speeds up as she approaches a slow moving defender is working to create a more advantageous momentum difference. All defenders

Figure 87 Winning a One-on-One

Beating defenders can be simplified to two steps — push the ball past and beat them to it. It sounds simple but it isn't. To beat the defender to the ball one must be fairly close. When you are close to the defender the ball is vulnerable and it isn't easy to push the ball past. In this photo the ball has been played into the space behind the defender and the attacker will easily beat her to it.

with a momentum different than the attacker are beatable.

A defender's stance or body position is important in one-on-ones. The basic defender's stance is balanced, with weight evenly distributed on both feet. From this stance the defender can move with equal ease in any direction. When the defender starts moving the weight is shifted to one leg which then becomes immobilized. The immobilized leg is unable to intercept the ball and the attacker can easily go by on that side. Fakes, stopping, starting and changing direction not only create momentum but temporarily immobilize defenders by disturbing the balanced stance. A good attacker learns to quickly read and respond to the subtle changes in stance that indicate vulnerability.

The importance of reaction time may be seen when approaching and going around a stationary defender. The stationary defender is easily beaten if you can push the ball past at the correct time. If you push the ball too soon the defender reacts and intercepts; wait too long and the defender is close and too big an obstacle. The timing is critical. The timing good dribblers possess is based on an instinctive feel for the effects of momentum and reaction time. To beat defenders we take advantage of, or create, conditions in which the defender will be unable to respond because of delays due to reaction time, momentum or stance.

Figure 88 Reading The Defender

Good dribblers are constantly reading their opposing defender. They perform an action and see if the defender's response is appropriate. The successful attacker monitors the defender's distance, momentum, foot position, balance, and attentiveness. Temporary weakness must be quickly exploited. Here, U.S. National Team Member April Heinrichs, one of the best women dribblers in the world, monitors a Swedish defender. (North America Cup Tournament, Blaine, Minnesota)

The Dribbling Cycle

Many players approach dribbling situations like they would gymnastics; they develop a single routine that they try to use for all situations. What works for gymnastics doesn't necessarily work in soccer. When defenders don't know their "part" and don't respond accordingly, the attempt fails. To become a good dribbler, one must develop tools (skills) and apply them with flexibility.

A one-on-one is a cycle in which one player acts and the opponent reacts. At each moment you must evaluate the response of the defender. This is called "reading" a defender. For example, approach close, fake a move in one direction, and watch the defender's response. If the defender falls for the fake and starts moving in one direction, you are free to move in the opposite direction. If your fake doesn't convince the defender, try something different. To beat a defender you must create a situation or take advantage of a condition in which the defender cannot react to prevent your passage. The basic cycle is to act, evaluate the reaction, and then do your next action (Fig. 88, pg. 77).

Easily Beatable Defenders
• Too close
• Too slow
• Approaching too fast
• Unskilled
• Ball-watcher

Table 15

Control

Control is an important aspect of dribbling. When the defender is in control, the attacker is responding to the defender, struggling to keep possession with few options. When the attacker is in control, the defender is responding to the attacker's changes of direction and fakes.

To gain control one of the players executes an action that requires a reaction by the opponent. Because a defender must respond to prevent goals, shots or shooting fakes are used by attackers to move defenders and establish control. Fakes and body position are used by defenders to gain control. The attacker needs control to successfully shoot, pass or dribble. A defender seeks control in the hope of gaining possession of the ball, forcing attackers to move in a particular direction, do something undesirable, or just to prevent them from doing what they want. To be successful in one-on-ones you must be a controller.

Easily Beatable Defenders

All defenders are beatable, but some are more easily beaten than others. The most easily "beatable" defenders have two things in common — they cannot respond in time to an attacker's action and there is space behind them. The inability to respond may be due to momentum, reaction time, inattentiveness, unbalanced stance or being slow (Table 15). Among the most common beatable types are those aggressive defenders who get too close or approach too quickly. They effectively remove the space that allows them time to evaluate and respond. Good dribblers develop an almost reflex recognition of all beatable defenders — quickly pushing the ball past them and proceeding on their way. Learn to view beatable defenders as golden opportunities. If you're confident, go out of your way to beat one: it's one of the best ways to create space and to confuse and demoralize opponents.

Beating Defenders with the Wall Pass

Getting the ball past a defender involves either dribbling or passing. The wall pass is a simple "two-pass" combination in which an attacker uses a teammate to quickly get past a defender. By using the teammate as a "wall", the attacker can ricochet the ball behind the defender and get to it first. Although seemingly easy, the play requires a teammate that understands the play, has passing skill, and is positioned in the right place at the right time (Fig. 56, pg. 48).

Approach to Aggressive Defenders

"If reckless, he can be killed; If quick-tempered you can make a fool of him." Sun Tzu

Aggressive defenders actively — and sometimes recklessly — approach the ball (Fig. 89, pg. 79), creating momentum useful to the attacker. This momentum can be used to take that defender temporarily out of the play by stepping aside at the proper moment, like a bullfighter (Fig. 85, pg. 75). How close an attacker should allow a defender to approach before stepping aside depends on how quickly the defender is moving. A defender approaching more slowly must be allowed to get closer than a defender who is rapidly approaching (Fig. 89, pg. 79).

Other variables also will make each situation different. A defender approaching with long strides is easier to beat than one using short steps — the defender taking short steps can change di-

Figure 89 Aggressive Defender

One of the first things a player must learn is how to avoid a reckless, aggressive defender. It is a tool of survival necessary not only for keeping the ball but also for avoiding injury. The key is the ability to cut the ball sideways quickly at the correct moment.

rection more quickly. The defender's angle of approach is also important. The defender who approaches head-on is easiest to avoid, since the attacker can dribble either to the right or the left. A defender approaching at an angle is more difficult to beat — there is little room to cut to the middle and the defender can cut the attacker off from balls played forward. Speed, stride length, and angle of approach are variables that make beating a high-pressure defender difficult.

Although fakes are difficult to remember and carry out, they are very effective against aggressive defenders. The approaching defender has little time to evaluate and often responds to even the subtlest fakes. A good fake often embar-

Figure 90 Fast Approach

If the defender's final approach to the ball is too fast the attacker can safely go to the side and around. The timing is critical. If the approach is slow the attacker must wait until the defender is close before making a move.

rasses a defender who "falls" for it; putting the attacker in control of the approaching defender. Fake early and use simple, quick fakes — such as a head-and-shoulder dip in one direction. Keep a few fakes in mind for aggressive defenders.

Some Types of Aggressive Defenders

Approach From the Middle

For an attacker near the sides of the field, a defender approaching from the middle is difficult to avoid. The most inviting but difficult option is a cut to the middle. This is almost impossible because of the defender's angle of approach (Fig. 91 & 92, pg. 81). Yet, by learning to play the ball behind you, this can be done (Fig. 93 to 95, pg. 82). Sometimes you can push the ball ahead, wait for the defender to go by, and then retrieve the ball. If the approaching defender will cross in front of you, you can stop the ball at the last moment so that the defender barrels by (Fig. 84, pg. 74).

Slow Approach

Defenders that use a slow final approach are difficult to beat because their momentum is small and doesn't take them out of the play. If they move with small steps, they also can thwart your attempts to go around them. Beat them

Figure 91 Sweeper Attack!

You have just beaten a defender and are racing down the flanks. Then, like a flash, another defender zooms toward you from the middle. This isn't just anyone, this is the best the defense has — Godzilla the Sweeper. She is smart. If you continue straight she will cut you off from the ball and probably knock you into the parking lot. If you try to cut, she's got the angle covered. For a more successful approach see the next page.

Figure 92 Sweeper Attack!

Figure 93 Mad Bull

This is another defender rapidly approaching from the middle. The defender's angle of approach is a good one. If the attacker continues straight he is destroyed. If he pushes the ball past the defender he won't be able to get to it. Cutting toward the middle is also very difficult because a traditional cut would lead to a collision so the attacker uses a trick to beat the defender. He steps over the ball and plays the ball to the middle with the trailing foot. In effect, he cuts the ball behind his body.

Figure 94 Mad Bull

Figure 95 Mad Bull

Figure 96 Cornered!

When you are stuck with a defender on your back, swallow your pride and pass. Sometimes this is difficult because you can't see teammates or you are in an area of the field where there is little room to support. The situation depicted in this series of photos is occurring in a corner of the defensive third of the field — there is no room. The player with the ball fakes a pass or sharp movement to the center and then safely reverses direction.

by waiting until they are close, and then moving quickly away at an angle. Because the timing is very difficult to master, this is a situation where it pays to have a fake (e.g., false start in one direction) up your sleeve.

Trapped in a Corner

Sometimes you get the ball in a corner, close to your goal, with an opponent on your back. Dribbling out may be your only option, because it is often unsafe to pass to the goalkeeper, and teammates have no room to come to your aid. You can sometimes beat the opponent by turning as if to go to the middle of the field, doing a stepover fake as if to pass to the keeper, then quickly cutting to the edge of the field and proceeding upfield (Fig. 96).

Double Trouble

Your approach to being double-teamed will depend on your options and how the defenders are positioned. Your best choice is to pass. If this is not possible or if your ego won't let you — take them on. If the defenders are side-by-side your best approach is to face them and try to go between (Fig. 97, pg. 83). If the defenders are staggered (one behind the other), but close, you may, if you

Figure 97 Double-Teamed

When you are being pressured by two defenders, passing is the best choice. However, if your adrenalin level is surging and you must defend your honor, face the defenders and try to split them. This guy could easily have passed the ball, but either his ego was involved or he didn't see or hear his teammate supporting in the background.

are fast, be able to accelerate around the side of both. If the defenders are staggered and far apart you may be able to beat each separately, provided you are tricky and have good ball control.

Pivot

Some aggressive defenders will try to circle you

Figure 98 Pivot

When an aggressive opponent comes around you for the ball, beat them by moving in a tight circle. Nudge the ball while you pivot around using the outside of the foot. When you have completed the circle, the defender will be neatly out of your way, behind you.

when you shield the ball. You can easily beat such defenders by moving in a quick, tight turning circle, using the outside of the foot to push the ball (Fig. 98, pg. 84). When finished, the defender will be on your back, and you will be free to move up the field.

Approaches to Passive Defenders

Rather than aggressively pursuing the ball, passive defenders patiently wait for you to make a mistake.

The passive defender allows you some space, maintains a balanced stance and attempts to minimize momentum differences by moving in the same direction at the same speed. You must remove the space, so they have little time to react, and create a momentum difference or unbalanced stance. Because these defenders are so difficult to beat, often the best advice is to pass. Whether you choose to dribble or to pass around the passive defender will depend on your ability, the tactical situation and the score. The average player should attempt to beat the defender only if that person is the final obstacle preventing a shot on goal.

The most common method of overcoming a passive defender is to accelerate at the defender, get the defender off balance, push the ball past and collect it (Fig. 101 to 103, pg. 86). This is easier said than done. As you approach, the ball must be in constant motion, keeping the defender guessing about where the ball will be next, since it is vulnerable to a sudden tackle. When you are

Figure 99 Nutmeg

In our simplified view of the dribbling task we must push the ball past the defender, then beat them to it. Getting the ball past the defender can be extremely difficult, particularly when the defender is close. However, if the defender takes a broad stance the ball can simply be passed through their legs. This humbling experience is called a "nutmeg". Use the inside-of-the-foot pass to push the ball through the legs when the defender is close. (continued...)

Figure 100 Nutmeg

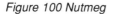

Look for the opportunity to nutmeg when the defender has a low, broad stance. You can encourage a wide stance by changing direction several times. The opportunity to nutmeg also occurs at the end of a fast defender's approach. In stopping, the defender will conveniently plant their legs far apart. (See Fig. 5, pg. 5.)

Figure 101 Passive Defender

The patient defender, the one that waits for you to move first, is difficult to beat. Passing is often the best option. To beat the defender you must close the distance, get them off balance, push the ball past, then beat them to it. In this series, the attacker closes the distance, fakes movement to the inside, and then goes by on the outside.

Figure 102 Passive Defender

Figure 103 Passive Defender

very close, use fakes and quick changes of direction to keep control and get the defender out of the path. You must watch the defender closely as these moves are applied, waiting for the moment when it is safe to go past. This cycle of action, evaluation and next action requires skill and confidence.

Sometimes passive defenders play with too broad a stance, practically inviting the attacker to send the ball neatly between their legs —this is called a "nutmeg" (Fig. 99 & 100, pg. 85). You must be close to defenders when you try this, so you can beat them to the ball. This "nutmeg" maneuver also requires passing accuracy and poise. You can sometimes create the opportunity to nutmeg by changing direction several times, forcing the defender into a broad-based stance. Aggressive approaching defenders also provide frequent opportunities to nutmeg (Fig. 5, pg. 5), since they tend to stop with widely spread legs. Look for the opportunity to "nutmeg"; it greatly demoralizes a defender.

Another way to create a momentum difference is by tempting a defender into trying to capture a seemingly exposed and vulnerable ball — "baiting" (Fig. 104, pg. 87). When the defender lunges for the bait — the ball — the attacker quickly carries it past the impatient defender. Successful baiting requires very quick feet.

Figure 104 Baiting

"Offer the enemy a bait or lure him; feign disorder and strike him." Sun Tzu

One method of beating an impatient defender is to "bait" them. The defender is tempted into making a rash move for the ball. The ball is "dangled" just within reach. When the impetuous opponent lunges for the ball, it is withdrawn and quickly pushed past. This trick requires quick feet and good ball movement skills.

Some Types of Passive Defenders

The Cone Defender

Cone defenders stand still, like traffic safety cones, as you run toward them (Fig. 105, pg. 89). They are both vulnerable and threatening, since they are usually thinking of stepping forward and taking the ball. The key to beating these defenders is to cut and go around them early — preferably just as they start forward. A common mistake is to wait a fraction of a second too long, losing the ball as the defender steps forward. If you keep the ball close and take short steps, you can respond quickly. Doing a fake before cutting also will help to control the defender. The secret to beating a living "cone" is to act early.

Defender "Sideways-On"

In the "sideways-on position", the defender is near the attacker's shoulder, facing the same direction (Fig. 106, pg. 89). Defenders often assume this position when defending on the flanks, or when defending fastbreaks in the middle of the field. Defenders choose this position because they can run more easily (useful on fastbreaks) and because along the sidelines they can prevent movement toward the middle. If you are fast you may out-run this type of defense, though the ball is a mild handicap. Another approach is to throw the defender off your shoulder by stopping, starting and using fakes(Fig. 195, pg. 182). When the defender has gotten ahead, you can cut to the middle. Also, when both players are moving very fast, the defender cannot prevent a sudden cut to the middle. A safer way out is to stop and reverse direction, pivoting out of danger. You can then either back pass or shield the ball and dribble across the field. A sideways-on defender should present no difficulties to an attacker that knows these techniques.

Defender Side-by-Side

All stop and start fakes are effective in beating defenders running side-by-side (Fig. 107, pg. 89 & Fig. 66, pg. 58). For example, when both dribbler and defender are running parallel, the scissors-move is often effective. To use it, the attacker steps over the ball with the foot that is closest to the defender. The defender gets the impression that the attacker is about to stop and therefore slows down. The inside of the attacker's opposite foot then carries the ball forward as the player accelerates, beating the defender (Fig. 196, pg. 183).

Figure 105 Cone Defender

If you are moving and the defender is standing still it is a situation filled with opportunity and danger. If you get past the defender they probably will not be able to recover in time to catch you. However, when they face you, as in this photo, they will probably suddenly and unexpectedly tackle. Keep the ball close, keep up your speed, do an early fake and cut early.

Figure 106 Sideways-On

A clever defender on your shoulder is difficult to beat. Their position prevents a cut to the middle and gives them a head-start in any race for the ball. However, if you are faster go for it. What to do? Often you can cut if you first do some stop and start fakes to back them up. If you are both moving quickly you can still cut because their momentum will carry them forward, preventing them from blocking you. You can also cut behind your body. Another option is to simply pivot back out of the whole mess. This is better than losing the ball.

Figure 107 Side by Side

The side-by-side position is similar to sideways-on. However, the defender is parallel, not ahead of you. The situation is often a simple foot-race for the ball. If you are faster, then you will be successful. If you are slower, use stop and start fakes to put the defender off your shoulder then cut to the middle.

Moving Defender

Sometimes, usually on a fastbreak, a defender will run in front of you, facing the same direction and watching you over one shoulder (Fig. 118, pg. 102). It's fun to beat this defender: you simply keep changing direction, cutting to the right, then to the left. Just when the defender has twisted to look at you over one shoulder, you cut the other way.

Making an Angle

Successfully beating defenders doesn't always require moving past them. To make shots on goal and through passes, an attacker only needs to get clear of the defender for a moment. The English call this process, "making an angle". You can "make an angle" by quick changes of direction or by using fakes.

Miscellaneous Circumstances

Loose Balls

Loose balls can result from many things — poor receiving skills, poor dribbling skills, tackles, rebounded shots, inaccurate or long passes, uneven ground, goalie punts, and other misfortunes. When two players arrive at a loose ground ball simultaneously (Fig. 108, pg. 90), the one whose body is most securely planted and has the greatest momentum will usually come away

Figure 108 Loose Balls

When two players are in a fifty-fifty situation with a loose ball between them the tendency of the inexperienced is to thrash blindly. Pushing the panic button never helps. This activity usually just creates another free ball. The proper action is to attempt to get possession. Hook the ball to the side and back where you can get to it first and shield it or use the sole of your foot to roll the ball back away from your opponent.

with the ball. If you have a chance at capturing a loose ball, direct it toward a space (Fig. 108, pg. 90), then make a long back pass to an open teammate to secure possession.

Resisting Leg Tackles

When you dribble through traffic, many defenders will extend a leg to swat the ball loose (Fig. 109, pg. 91). You can keep possession by leaning slightly forward and planting both feet solidly behind the ball, absorbing casual leg tackles. By reacting quickly in this way a dribbler can advance safely through heavy traffic. Of course, players with very quick feet can avoid the tackles entirely.

Figure 109 Surviving Leg Tackles

A defender that idly sticks one leg out in an attempt to get the ball should not succeed. They won't if you crouch, lean forward, and plant yourself squarely behind the ball when the attempt is made. The tackling leg should simply bounce off the ball. Players with quick feet can often avoid the tackling leg entirely.

Individuals and the Team

Your team's tactical approach should influence the decisions that you make as an individual. Some examples of team tactics that could potentially influence you include: choosing to play two- or one-touch, to play short passes, to dribble around the last line of defenders, to attempt quick counter-attacks, to use more back passes and to play a possession style. There will be times when you won't have the option of implementing these tactics due to your immediate situation. However, when you have the time, opportunity and options, keep in mind your team's approach to the game.

Chapter 4

Team Tactics

Table 16

"He who takes his opponent lightly will fall." Sun Tzu

"What the multitude cannot comprehend is how victory may be produced for them out of the enemy's tactics." Sun Tzu

Summary: A coach must recognize and exploit the inherent weakness of an opponent's defense. A system of individual markings must be thrown into disarray by radical movements and beating defenders; the cracks in zones must be exploited by short passing; the space away from bunches used; reckless aggression countered by skilled dribbling; and the offsides trap countered by dribbling or careful passes behind the defense. There are many other factors that affect a team's approach to a game, including: the size of the field, the nature of the field's surface, weather, time of day and even the nature of the attending crowd.

Why Open Players Exist

A team's overall approach to a game is its team tactics. These are actions that, taking into consideration the game conditions and the opponent, make best use of a team's assets while protecting its weaknesses. Team tactics influence each individual, and are implemented by the decisions of each individual on a team. For example, a team policy of rapid, short passing requires the cooperation of every player on the team. This level of cooperation requires a degree of discipline found only in the best teams. For this reason, most team tactics must be kept simple.

Figure 110 Why Open Players Exist

If you were to ask the defending team in this photo why the attacker on the right was able to score you would probably get lots of finger-pointing and excuses. In fact, a goal is usually the result of many mistakes. In this situation, the player with the ball is now open because they have beaten their marking defender (arrow 1). The defenders in the penalty box are currently disorganized and confused. They are also ball-watching — not checking the space behind them. The player that should be covering the open attacker on the right (arrow 2) is a forward, that doesn't see defense as part of his responsibility. This is an excellent example of an attacking player recognizing a space and making a well-timed run.

Open players exist: 1) because of the intrinsic nature of an opponent's defensive system, 2) because defenders are beaten, 3) because of defensive disorganization, 4) and because of miscellaneous factors (fatigue, sudden turnovers, etc.).

"One who sets the entire army in motion to chase an advantage will not attain it." Sun Tzu

The team with one more player around the ball theoretically has an advantage. This player is, in theory, open and therefore useful, creating what is called a "numerical advantage". However, when there are five or more players near the ball, one extra player near the ball doesn't help and has very little useful time. The most useful numerical advantage is gained from turning a one-vs.-one situation into a two-vs.-one, or converting a two-vs.-two into a three-vs.-two. The most useful players for creating this numerical advantage come from behind the ball moving forward unnoticed and unmarked (Fig. 110).

* Win One-on-Ones

* Take Defenders for a Hike

* Use Frequent Switching Movements

Table 17

Because of Defensive Tactics

"To anticipate the enemy's strategy his methods must be studied. Determine the enemy's plans and you will know which strategy will be successful and which will not." Sun Tzu

Everything in life seems to have advantages and disadvantages, including different approaches to team defense. For example, a pressure-type defense often succeeds in getting the ball back but occasionally gives up easy goals. A retreating defense offers greater security close to goal but doesn't cover opponents far from goal, thus allowing the opponent to keep possession easily. Successful tactics must take into account the strengths and weaknesses of a defense. The attacking team's approach should exploit opportunities those tactics create.

Individual Markings

"Placing strength against weakness is the most important principle in war." Sun Tzu

With individual markings ("man-on-man") each defender covers an individual attacker. Individual markings may be applied to a particular individual on a team, to a specific area of the field (the scoring area), or to a team as a whole. It can be very effective if done well. Fortunately for the offense, a system of individual markings is always vulnerable to good dribblers. Whenever possible, strong attackers should be matched against weak defenders. Skilled dribblers should be encouraged to beat marking defenders. This forces other defenders to abandon coverage — destroying the marking system.

If your team doesn't have the dribbling skill, increased offensive movements are important. It helps if one understands traditional defensive organization. Like traditional offense (using formations), players on defense have an area of responsibility that corresponds to their position. Any defensive player will feel uncomfortable if they stray from that position. To remove a marking defender take them far from their home turf. Move! Switch sides. Go from the front to the back. Do takeovers and switching movements.

Tight markings create opportunities to beat defenders by passing. When tightly covered, you can often beat the defender to a ball played into space. This is an example of how a certain tactic (individual markings) will not only create problems but also opportunities.

Zone Markings

"And when he prepares everywhere he will be weak every-where." Sun Tzu

In zone defensive systems, defenders are responsible for covering designated areas. A zone system, in theory, denies the attacking team large areas of space. Fortunately, this system creates many smaller areas of space. Therefore a useful tactic, for a team with the skill, is to use short one-touch passes to take advantage of these small spaces. The rapid passing also exploits another feature common to zone defenses — confusion and slow organization. However, if the opponent also bunches, these tactics may only have limited success.

Figure 111 Bunch

A defensive team that bunches around the ball is vulnerable to rapid changes in the field of play, as illustrated here. To deliberately create large spaces such as this by bunching is an unused offensive tactic. If the bunch forms too close to the ball it is extremely difficult to change the field of play. The open player at the bottom of the picture could have more space and time by being closer to the edge of the field.

Beating the Defensive Shell

- Quick Counterattacks

- Draw Out Defense

- Penetrate Shell

  - Air Attack
  - Dribbling
  - Short Passing

Table 18

Beating Pressure Tactics

- Plan ahead

- Avoid playing the ball too long in one area

- Always pass to players with large amounts of space

- Play the ball one-touch when pressured (if you have the skill)

- Beat aggressive defenders when there is room and when you have the skill

- Create uncertainty by using fakes

- Run through after passing

- Keep the ball on the ground for faster control

Table 19

Bunching

"In war, numbers alone confer no advantage." Sun Tzu

"To strengthen a point, another must be weakened." Sun Tzu

It is common policy to seek a numerical advantage in the area of the ball and in the goal area. Any time a team is thick in some area it is thin in another. In other words, there is space away from the bunch (Fig. 111, pg. 96). A defensive team that clearly bunches around the ball is vulnerable to rapid changes in the field of play. The quickest method is the long crossing pass. Other methods include redistributing the ball to the far space by crossfield dribbling, by shorter passes or by an initial back pass (Fig. 65, pg. 56). Although bunches create opportunities, in reality it is difficult to profit. The intense pressure in the bunch causes ball-watching and often the space is not seen. Even if noticed, pressure and limited passing angles make moving the ball difficult (Fig. 63, pg. 54).

Defensive Shell

"For if he prepares to the front his rear will be weak, and if to the rear, his front will be fragile..." Sun Tzu

Where a defensive team chooses to make its stand affects where space can be found. A defensive team that pushes forward, attempting to keep an attacking team in its own end, will create an exploitable area of space at its back. Use of the offsides trap also does this. On the other hand, a defensive team that sets up its defense close to goal ("shells up"), only offers space away from goal. Each approach creates its own tactical opportunities.

Teams that withdraw into a defensive shell around their goal can be difficult to beat. The best offensive approach is to develop attacks quickly before the defense can retreat (Table 18). To do this it is often necessary to draw out the defense first. This can be done by retreating and setting up one's own defense very deep. Otherwise, a team can attempt to draw out the defense by playing possession soccer with many back passes. A disciplined defense still will not leave their shell. If all else fails, penetrate by kicking high balls into the middle. As the English say, "Get wide and get quality crosses across the front of the goal." This may be successful with attackers skilled at handling air balls, or if the opponents are weak at clearing. Attempts to penetrate the shell on the ground are more difficult due to the crowding, but may be worth an attempt if a team has good dribbling and short-passing skills.

Pressure

General Measures

Using high pressure is a common defensive tactic. Techniques to increase pressure include: aggressive individual play, tight individual markings, and restricting the attacking space (e.g., by use of the offsides rule). Pressure is a lack of time. To overcome pressure we must do everything possible to have more time (space), and when that is not possible we must do things more quickly (Table 19).

There are many ways to provide more time. Plan your actions before receiving the ball and you won't have to use time thinking later. Keep the ball on the ground so it takes less time to control and can be played more quickly and accurately. Stay spread out to have more time and decrease pressure near the ball. When pressured be more careful about pass selection, choose only players with enough time for their skill level. When a teammate receives a pass, move to support very early and communicate your presence before they are pressured.

Figure 112 Individual Pressure
Pressure is a universal defensive tactic. It is successful largely because players don't have the necessary skills or tactical sophistication to overcome it. To overcome pressure a team must optimize its use of space. That is, passes should be made to players with sufficient time to control the ball before being pressured. Dribbling should be limited to areas of space. Passing should be rapid, using the whole field. Players should sprint to space after passing seeking to complete combination plays. Reckless defenders should be beaten when possible, in uncrowded areas. These tactics will frustrate, discourage and exploit defensive pressure tactics.

Beating Offsides Defense

- Attack last line of defenders

  - Wall passes
  - Dribbling
  - Passes with runs to space behind the defense

- Overlapping runs when the defense pushes forward

Table 20

Individual Pressure

"Victory is found in relation to the foe you are facing." Sun Tzu

If you have the skills, the surest way to discourage individual, pressuring defenders is by beating them with dribbling or wall passes. Skilled dribblers easily beat highly aggressive defenders. However, use dribbling only against isolated defenders and not when in a bunch. It is good advice to beat one defender then pass. Also, wall passes become effective tools when the defender is too close. Learn to see aggressive defenders not just as problems, but opportunities.

If you lack the skill or confidence to beat an aggressive defender, you have several other options. Perhaps the best option is to pass the ball one-touch. This requires planning — knowing ahead of time where to pass. When this is not possible or desirable, use fakes to throw off the pressuring defender. Sprinting through after passing, which creates the opportunity to beat the defender with a wall pass, also helps to keep aggressive defenders at bay.

Team Pressure

With aggressive teams, individual defenders focus on the ball and move toward it. They become bunching, ball watchers. Since it is difficult to exploit this situation, it is better to avoid it. The offensive team should restrict dribbling since this greatly aggravates the problem. Only try to beat isolated defenders in uncrowded areas. Otherwise, dribble only when it is necessary for maintaining possession, for changing the field of play and when there is one defender to beat for a shot on goal.

Passing restrictions are also necessary when playing against an aggressive team. Avoid making too many short passes in the same area — by the third pass there is a crowd. There must be a mixture of short and long passes; three short passes and a long pass that changes fields is a good pattern. This pattern is also useful as it helps exploit the weakness of this defense — ignoring the space away from the ball. An aggressive team not only creates problems but opportunities for those with the proper tactics.

Use of the Offsides Rule

A high pressure defense often accompanies use of the offsides rule. When seeking to exploit the offsides rule, the last defenders play in a line across the field. The line itself and coordinated movements by the line often trap for-

Figure 113 Beating Offsides

The defense is vulnerable any time it is playing in a flat line across the field, as when the defense attempts to take advantage of the offsides rule. There is undefended space behind the defense, and the defenders are poorly positioned to back each other up if someone is beaten. The most direct approach to exploiting these weaknesses is to attack the defensive line by dribbling. If you beat your marking defender, particularly if you attack a central defender, other defenders will have a hard time stopping you.

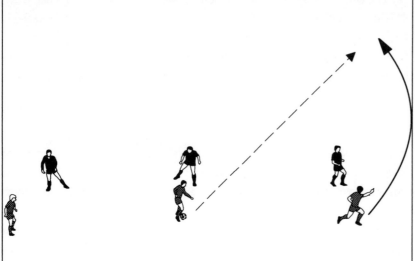

Figure 114 Passing to Beat Flat Defense

When the defense is flat (in a line straight across the field), it has trouble covering the space that exists behind it. Use this space by making a pass to a player running into it. The run must be precisely timed. It must start from an "on-side" position.The run can only be made when the player with the ball is ready and "head up". The slightest hint of a forward movement by the player making the run should trigger the pass. The pass can go first if it has the right pace and the passer is certain that the runner can beat their marking defender.

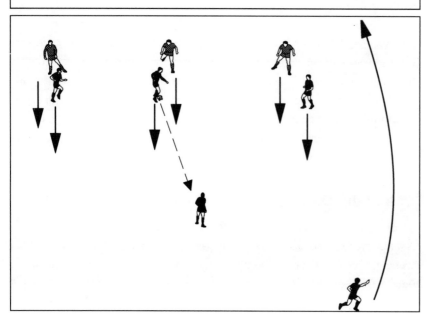

Figure 115 Overlapping to Beat Offsides Trap

When the defense uses the offsides rule it plays in a line that frequently moves forward to trap attackers in "offsides" positions, creating turnovers. The defensive line usually moves forward whenever the ball moves back, such as when the attacking team back-passes. Knowing this, the attacking team can run players forward from well behind the ball, just as the defense is pushing up. If a pass is made behind the defense as the overlapping attacker approaches the defensive line, the overlapper should have no trouble reaching it first, and continuing to goal unmolested.

wards in offside positions; a freekick is awarded the defending team for this offensive rule infraction. Though there is a large potential space for the offense behind the defense, use of the offsides rule restricts the offense to a much smaller space in front of the defense. This lack of space greatly limits offensive movements and creates ball control problems — more turnovers.

The team seeks to minimize the effects of these defensive tactics and exploit the opportunities created. The team minimizes the effects of the offsides trap by making players very conscious of being in an offsides position. This requires specific practice.

Figure 116 Offsides Defense Beaten

A well-timed offsides trap can be a very effective defensive tool, creating many turnovers. It is a tactic associated with a certain risk, because a large space is created behind the defense. This risk is compounded by the lack of a deep player (sweeper) to pick up through balls and cover for defensive mistakes. These photos illustrate a goal being scored when the offsides trap is beaten.

Figure 117 Offsides Defense Beaten

The team exploits two weaknesses of the offsides defense — there are no defenders backing up the last defensive line and there is a large space behind the defense. The team uses the lack of defensive back-up (support) by encouraging players to attack the last line of the defense. A player with the ball that beats one defender in the last line has beaten the whole defense. The team dribbles (Fig. 113, pg. 100) and uses wall passes to do this. The team exploits the space behind the defense by well-timed and coordinated passes (Fig. 114, pg. 100) and runs into the space. These are very difficult, as the timing must be very precise to avoid an offsides foul.

In another tactic, attackers positioned behind the ball run forward whenever the defense pushes up. These attackers start running toward the space behind the defense (Fig. 115, pg. 100), beating the defense to any ball played into the space behind them. This works because the defenders are busy pushing forward with their offsides trap and cannot turn and change direction quickly.

Why a Badly Organized Defense
• Ignorance of defensive tasks
• Poor communication
• Poor vision — ball watching
• Poor discipline
• Poor concentration
• Fatigue

Table 21

Because of Beaten Defenders

"Invincibility lies in the defense; the possibility of victory in the attack." Sun Tzu

The most direct way to create open players is by beating defenders, gaining access to the space behind the defender. Another defender usually moves to help, creating defensive confusion and other open attackers. Defenders are commonly beaten because they are slow, inattentive, or matched against a more skilled opponent.

Figure 118 Fastbreak
Each defensive tactic creates the opportunity for different offensive tactics. There is no perfect defense. The opportunity for fastbreaks or breakaways is created by any defense that has sufficient space behind it. Defenses that attempt to confine opponents to the area around their goal or defenses that use the offsides rule are particularly vulnerable. To successfully take advantage of the offensive opportunity requires the right tools — fast players that want to score and field players and a goalkeeper that see opportunities. It is important to push the attack as rapidly as possible and conclude with a shot. Notice the defenders sprinting back.

Decreased Movements

Consequences:

- Poorer support (more turnovers, more vulnerable to pressure)
- Fewer open players and passing options
- Poorer penetration (fewer scoring chances)
- Inability to take advantage of opportunities
- Severer consequences when possession is lost

Decreased ability to perform skill-related activities

Consequences:

- Increased turnovers from poor receiving, bad passing, bad dribbling
- Decreased scoring

Mental Changes

- Decreased motivation
- Emotional lability
- Decreased concentration

Consequences:

- Fewer open players
- Open players are not seen
- Turnovers
- Poor communication
- Less cooperation
- Mistakes in judgement
- Poorer field vision

Because of Poor Defensive Organization

A poorly organized or slow to organize defense causes open players. Poor defensive organization results from: 1) ignorance of defensive tasks, 2) poor communication between defenders, 3) poor vision — ball watching, 4) poor discipline in maintaining markings, 5) poor concentration, and 6) fatigue.

Creating defensive confusion creates open attackers by disrupting defensive organization. Radical attacking movements and beating defenders are the best tools to create confusion. Beat individual defenders at the ball by dribbling or combination play. Beat defenders covering away from the ball by well-synchronized through passes. Use radical crossfield or back-to-front-to-back movements to create confusion, not slow, wimpy movements in one area of the field. Rapid switching movements, fakes, runs to create space, and rapid pass-move combinations also increase confusion. All of these things should be normal parts of a team's pattern of play.

Miscellaneous Factors

"Keep him under a strain and wear him down." Sun Tzu

Defensive fatigue creates open attackers because tired defenders are more easily beaten, can't maintain their markings and can't get back in time to help their teammates. Open attackers temporarily exist after each sudden turnover because it takes defenders time to get back and get organized. This is a normal, unavoidable risk resulting from pushing players forward and making runs.

Common Offensive Patterns

The Fastbreak

"The ultimate tactical weapon is surprise." Sun Tzu

Although soccer is a varied and unpredictable game it has certain recurrent patterns. For example, one team may play possession soccer, controlling the ball for long periods, while the opponent periodically launches quick counterattacks. In spite of one team's seeming dominance, the score may be close or the counterattacking team may win.

Rapid counterattacks into the space behind the defense characterize the fastbreak offense (Fig. 118, pg. 102). The attack usually starts from a turnover in midfield or from the goalie quickly delivering the ball upfield. A team must recognize fastbreak opportunities and quickly initiate the attack. The space behind the defense is used by accurate through passes or by fast dribbling attackers. In either case speed is an essential ingredient. Use this offense against the offsides defense, against pressure defenses and against a retreating defense — whenever there is significant space behind the defense.

Possession Offense

Patient offensive buildups, using frequent square and back passes, characterize the possession-style offense. To play this style a team must have excellent support, movement, communication and passing skills. Use it to draw out a team that retreats and sets up their defense close to the penalty area. Use this style when ahead to consume time. Use possession tactics in combination with one-touch passing to frustrate and neutralize an extremely aggressive team.

"Both advantage and danger are inherent in maneuver." Sun Tzu

A possession-style offense has several disadvantages. In building the attack a possession offense gets drawn out and becomes vulnerable to the quick counterattack. A team also can get preoccupied with pretty passing and never get scoring opportunities. Goals count — not minutes of possession or passing numbers.

Figure 119 Field Conditions

Bad playing conditions, whether they are due to wind, rain or rough playing surface, affect both offense and defense on both teams. In general, the worse the conditions the more effective is a simple offensive style. With standing water, ground passing and dribbling become unreliable means of advancing the ball.

Tips on Decreasing Turnovers

- Practice fundamental skills.

- Don't attempt things beyond your capabilities.

- Keep the ball on the ground.

- Don't keep the ball too long.

- Keep the ball moving.

- Look! Plan ahead! Know all your options.

- Don't turn unless safe or acceptable risk.

- Don't panic. When you have few passing options, go back and find someone safe.

- Communicate with players under pressure.

- Move to create passing options for the player with the ball.

- When covered, move.

Decreasing Unnecessary Turnovers

In a game where taking risks is necessary for success, losing possession of the ball is to be expected. However, there are things that can be done to decrease the number of unnecessary turnovers. Preventable turnovers are a result of inadequate skill, poor decision making and having few options.

Skill is a primary determinant of success in anything that is attempted in soccer. A player with a high skill level has more options — can attempt more things and expect to be successful at them. Turnovers are created when players attempt things (e.g., beating a defender, making a perfect 50 yard pass) that are beyond their abilities. Players most frequently attempt impossible things when they are under pressure and see no easier options. These types of turnovers can be decreased by developing better skill, better vision, better communication, and by being patient. Instead of panicking and making "hope" ("I hope it gets there") passes, turn and dribble back into safe space. Make an easy pass to someone with a different perspective on the situation.

Many turnovers are a result of poor judgement or decision making. For example, turnovers frequently happen when a player decides to keep the ball too long. When you keep the ball too long the defense will not only gang-up on you but many of your passing options will disappear as nearby players are covered. The same thing happens when the ball is played too long in the same area — opportunities dry up. In addition, if you are dribbling with the ball you frequently get tunnel-vision and cannot see new options. If you have a good passing option use it. Don't wait for something better. Look and keep the ball moving — using the whole field.

We turn the ball over because we don't have safe passing options. This is a team problem. Players must move to provide right, left, and through options. When players in those positions are covered they must move and be replaced by others. When these movements aren't taking place a player will have few good options and may try something foolhardy. These types of turnovers are decreased by drilling players in the fundamental movements of support.

Other Factors in Team Tactics

"Know the enemy, know yourself; your victory will never be endangered. Know the ground, know the weather; your victory will then be total." Sun Tzu

Field size dictates how much space is available — greatly influencing a game. With less space, attacking on a small field is more difficult. Conversely, offense is generally easier on a larger field.

Field shapes affect styles of play. Long narrow fields provide good opportunities for the long downfield pass, with fast forwards sprinting to beat defenders to through balls. The type of field that favors a more patient, longer developing, "possession" style offense is long and wide. By contrast, small fields favor the quick counterattack because they are more easily defended.

"And as water has no constant form, there are in war no constant conditions." Sun Tzu

Wet weather (Fig. 119, pg. 104) creates slippery problems for both offense and defense, but bad weather handicaps the offense more seriously. Offense requires ball control and skill-related moves that can be thwarted by wind, puddles, bumps and other hazards. As conditions worsen, the offensive style must become simpler. Short passing becomes particularly unreliable as an offensive tool. Use fewer and longer passes. A skilled dribbler may still be effective provided they stay out of " lakes and ponds".

Wet grass and puddles often stop ground balls, so use air balls more. Trapping is a problem because balls skip and are hard to judge. Dribbling through puddles is also extremely difficult. To advance the ball through a puddle use short, shuffling, duck-footed steps. On wet fields shoot at every opportunity, since goalies have particular difficulty blocking low, skidding shots.

A rough playing surface creates passing, dribbling and ball control difficulties. Players should try to play around the rough spots when possible, although this is hard to remember during a game. One offensive advantage to rough fields is that low shots over rough ground are likely to present problems for goalies.

In a high wind the ball should be kept low, preferably on the ground, where the wind velocity is less. A strong tailwind makes it difficult to judge where balls played into the air will land. Some teams find they play better going into the wind since keeping the ball on the ground improves their control and speeds up their play. The wind usually is greatest in mid-afternoon, decreasing in the evening. Base the decision of whether to face the wind in the first or second half, on how strong it is and whether it might change.

A low sun can disturb player and goalie vision. It may be a factor in choosing an end of the field at the start of a game. When choosing between the advantage of the wind or the sun, most consider playing with the wind a greater advantage than having the sun in the opponent's eyes.

Whether to take an advantage during the first or second half of the game is controversial. Consider how great the advantage is, whether the advantage will disappear, and how strongly the team usually plays in the second half. Some coaches use an advantage in the second half, because then their team is more familiar with the opponent. Others feel strongly about having a first-half advantage, believing that it is easier to defend a lead than to overcome one.

Referees (Fig. 120, pg. 108) can definitely influence the outcome of a game. A coach or a team captain can make certain tactful requests of the referee. For example, if an opponent is playing in a very aggressive, potentially dangerous fashion, ask the referee to call plays more closely. If referees do not heed your advice they may be potentially liable for injuries. It may be useful to alert referees and linesmen of plans to use the offsides trap.

Every team must expect referees to occasionally make mistakes that adversely affect the outcome of a game. Emotional tantrums by coach or players in response to a referee's mistakes are rarely anything but counter-productive. If coaches learn to use discretion — talking to referees only infrequently, calmly, respectfully, and when correct — they will gain both respect and influence in return. In time, coaches become acquainted with individual referees and referees learn about teams and their coaches.

A large, partisan crowd is usually an intangible — but very effective — asset to a team. Players often perform dramatically better with parents or friends present. Strong support at an away game may help neutralize the "home" advantage. Like most psychological factors, the effect of the crowd is difficult to predict or control.

Figure 120 Referees (Photo by Kingsley LaBrosse)

Chapter 5

Defending at the Ball

"Anciently, the skillful warriors first made themselves invincible and awaited the enemy's moment of vulnerability." Sun Tzu

Summary: The heart of the defense is the individual defending at the ball. If this player is good the defense is secure. If this defender is weak other defenders are insecure, markings must be loose and the defense is vulnerable. The defender marking at the ball's job is to impede progress toward the goal and not get beaten in the process. Getting the ball back is not the primary objective. The defender tries to match the attacking player's momentum and use space for a buffer zone. The defender decreases the space when the attacker is moving away from goal. The basic defensive stance is evenly balanced, with knees bent, weight forward on the toes and eyes on the ball. Be cautious about tackling for there are few things worse than going for the ball and missing. Double-teaming an attacker can be effective and safe when in certain areas of the field and when an attacker has their head down. Use high and low pressure delaying techniques when outnumbered and when faced with a fastbreaking attacker.

The Importance of the Individual Defender

The worst mistake you can make on defense (other than scoring an "own goal") is to be beaten. If you are defending at the ball and the attacker dribbles around you this may start a cascade of events that leads to a goal. Someone else must mark at the ball, usually creating an unmarked attacking player free to receive a pass. This open player may then dribble or score.

109

A beaten defender also can mean a sharp shift in numerical advantage — for example, a two-on-two situation quickly becomes a two-on-one. The chances of scoring increase dramatically.

An unskilled defender must be backed up by positioning nearby teammates to cover. Backing up a defender decreases a teammate's effectiveness in marking opponents, leaving nearby attackers open to receive passes. This is not good. If, on the other hand, each defender is good, the teammates can relax a little and mark players around the ball more closely, hindering the passing game. The attacker's perspective is to say, "the dribbling game helps make the passing game". The defenders say, "stopping the dribbling game stops the passing game".

Objectives of Defender at Ball
• Impede progress of ball toward goal
• Regain possession of the ball
• Force attacker to watch the ball
• Encourage movement away from goal

Table 22

Objectives of the Individual Defender

The primary objective of the defender at the ball is to prevent goals and movement of the ball toward goal (Table 1). The tasks are: prevent the attacker from going around you, prevent shots on goal, and prevent through passes. The most difficult of these tasks is preventing shots on goal and through passes. These only require that the attacker push the ball to the side and be clear for an instant (Fig. 121, pg. 110).

Many coaches mistakenly teach that the primary objective of defenders is to get the ball back. This is a secondary objective. A defender whose objective is to get the ball will defend differently — playing aggressively and taking chances. Skilled attackers beat reckless, aggressive defenders and score goals.

Figure 121 Defender's Task

Simply defined, the defender's primary task is to inhibit movement of the ball toward goal. This not only involves blocking shots but also preventing through passes. Getting the ball back is a secondary task.

Therefore, getting the ball back is usually a secondary objective. An exception is when the team is behind late in a game, and desperately needs to score.

To prevent goals and movement of the ball toward goal, the defender need only serve as a constant obstacle between the ball and the goal — a constant wall. By placing their body between the ball and goal, the defender is not only blocking shots and through passes, but encouraging movement away from the goal.

To keep from being beaten the defender seeks to establish a "neutral situation". The defender plays off the attacker and moves in the same direction with the same speed — minimizing momentum differences. The separating space gives the defender time to evaluate and appropriately respond to the attacker's movements. In a "neutral situation" neither player has much of an advantage, so a "standoff" exists.

Another objective of the defender at the ball is to force the attacker to watch the ball (Fig. 122, pg. 111). The defender's close presence forces an unskilled attacker to watch the ball. An attacker watching the ball is chained to it, worried about protecting it. Such a person can't see offensive opportunities, makes mistakes, and finally loses the ball.

The defender applies pressure and establishes control by decreasing the attacker's space and limiting their options. One method of seizing the initiative and turning the attacker into a ball watcher is by tackling fakes. But be careful! You can be beaten when executing an exaggerated fake puts you off balance.

Figure 122 Pressuring the Attacker

Applying pressure at the ball involves decreasing the attacker's space. This must be done in a cautious manner because a hasty defender is easily beaten. Pressure may cause the player with the ball to lose it, to make an errant pass or to make other mistakes. One defensive objective is to force the attacker to watch the ball. The attacker is then unable to see passing options or the approach of a second defender (good time to double-team). The attacker becomes isolated and vulnerable.

There are many mistakes that result in beaten defenders. A defender playing too aggressively or too closely is vulnerable to a sudden change of direction, a fake, or a sudden burst of speed. The defender does not have time to react to the offensive action.

Differences in momentum are just as dangerous. A standing defender is vulnerable to a fast approaching attacker. The defender can't possibly accelerate fast enough to catch the attacker if they get past. The defender must start moving before the attacker gets close to minimize the momentum difference or else make an all-or-nothing attempt at the ball. The decision to tackle is based mostly on the speed of the defender and the attacker's ball control. A fast defender may turn and run with the attacker, a slow defender should tackle. If the dribbler is pushing the ball too far, is having trouble controlling the ball, or is not watching the defender, then tackling is better.

Defending as the Ball is Received

A defender marking a player receiving a ball has decisions to make: attempt to intercept, tackle ("destroy possession"), prevent the attacker from turning, or play off. There are many factors that will influence the decision: the area of the field, the proximity of teammates, the skill and speed of the defender, and the score.

The greatest influence on a defender's action toward an attacker receiving the ball is their distance from the receiving player. Try to rapidly decrease this distance while the ball is in flight ("make up ground"). Ideally, if you are

Figure 123 To Prevent Turning

An attacker receiving the ball facing their own keeper is vulnerable. The attacker will have limited vision and not be able to see approaching defenders — a good time to double-team. In turning, the attacker frequently exposes and loses the ball. The marking defender must be careful not to play too tightly or too loosely. The attacker can pivot around a defender that is too tight and turn easily in front of one that is too loose.

close enough, you can step through and intercept the pass. If this isn't possible, but you can arrive before the attacker controls the ball and gets their head up, then consider tackling. The tackle usually creates a loose ball ("destroying possession") but doesn't result in possession for the defending team (Fig. 124 & 125, pg. 113).

If the attacker is facing their defensive end, try to prevent them from turning (Fig. 123, pg. 112). This can be very difficult. Stand several feet behind the attacker. Don't be too close or the attacker can pivot, screen the ball and beat you. While turning, the attacker will often expose the ball for you to step

Figure 124 Intercept, Tackle, Play Off

The marking defender's actions as their opponent receives the ball will depend on their position when the ball is passed. If the defender is close, stepping through to intercept a pass is best. When this is not possible, the defender would like to tackle as the ball is received. If the defender is farther away and can't arrive before the ball is controlled, it still may be possible to keep the attacker from turning (Fig. 123). When still farther away, the final approach must be slow and cautious (Fig. 126 to 129).

Figure 125 Intercept, Tackle, Play Off

forward and take. But be careful — you may not be able to stop a skilled attacker from turning.

The attacker that has time to control the ball, turn and get their head up is another special problem. Don't approach too quickly or out of control. You can move quickly to a distance of nine or ten feet, but the final approach must be slow with quick, short steps and constant concentration on the ball (Fig. 126 to 129, pg. 115). Partly turn your body so your legs are ready to move quickly should the attacker suddenly sprint forward. The stance is the same as a track person might use when making a standing start in a race.

Figure 126 Final Approach

An attacker in control of the ball, with their head up, must be approached with caution. The initial approach to about 10 feet can be rapid, but at this distance the defender slows down. The final approach, to a distance of 3 to 6 feet, is made slowly with rapid, short steps.

Figure 127 Final Approach

(Sequence continued on following page.)

A defender moves from the center to mark an attacker moving down the flanks like merging with traffic on a freeway. If possible, approach fast-moving attackers coming down the center of the field in the same way. Take up a position to one side of the attacker's path and then gradually accelerate and "merge" as the attacker nears. Move to a position on their shoulder and guide them away from the scoring area in the center of the field.

Figure 128 Final Approach

(Caption on previous page.)

Figure 129 Final Approach

(Caption on previous page.)

Intercepting Passes

To intercept more passes, watch the eyes of the player with the ball — their last glance often betrays their target. Fool the attacker by covering your opponent loosely, creating a seemingly safe passing option. After the attacker has made their betraying glance, their next look is at the ball, concentrating on the pass. When their head goes down move forward, decreasing the receiver's space and positioning for an interception (Fig. 130, pg. 116).

Anticipation also leads to pass interceptions. To anticipate a pass you must understand the offensive tactical situation and what the attacker should do under the circumstances. In this way, many wall passes and through passes behind the defense can be read and intercepted.

Once an interception is made your next action is very important (Fig. 131 & 132, pg. 117). If you have moved forward into space to make the interception, continue forward, quickly counterattacking. If there is a good through pass, make it, otherwise dribble. If you were moving backward (or you just received an unexpected loose ball) think of safety, of securing possession of the ball. Your best choice is a long back pass, often to the keeper. Pass nicely to your keeper, to the side of the goal. Don't pass when they are close and advancing rapidly toward you (unless you like "own goals"). Screen the ball and let them scoop it up.

Figure 130 Intercepting Passes

The ability to anticipate passes comes with experience. However, an attacker's eyes and body positioning can give valuable clues. Before passing a player usually looks at the intended recipient, then down at the ball. Seeing the impending pass, a marking defender can quickly decrease the recipient's space when the passer looks down, increasing the chances of an interception.

The Defender's Use of Space

The amount of space given the attacker will vary. The space is a time buffer that allows you to evaluate attacker intentions and respond appropriately. The amount of space will vary with the opponent and the situation. There is danger in giving too much space and in giving too little. An attacker with too much space can dribble, complete through passes, or attempt shots on goal. With too little space, you may be easily beaten.

The ability of the opponent greatly influences the amount of space you allow. When defending against Sam Super Speed, there is need for more time than when defending against Sammy Slow. Tammy Tricky also must be given more

Figure 131 Having Made the Interception
Often a defender does a wonderful job of intercepting a pass or winning the ball, only to turn around and lose possession. This usually happens because a player tries to do too much after winning possession. Once possession is gained, the most important thing is to secure it, not to attempt something spectacular. With that in mind, the best thing to do with an intercepted pass or loose ball is to find someone safe, and get them the ball. Usually that safe person is a player with space, behind you. (continued)

Figure 132 Having Made the Interception

So, make a long back pass after getting a loose ball or intercepting a pass. The only exception is when you step forward to make an interception. Then it is often easy to continue forward, and launch a quick counter-attack. In this two photo series, a defender intercepts an attempted wall pass, and does the right thing, makes a back pass — in this case, to the goalkeeper.

space than Dana Dull. The amount of space safely allowed will be a unique reflection of the relative abilities of the attacker and defender. Learn about your opponents. Know which ones you can safely pressure; they represent opportunities to create turnovers. Pressure better players only when it is safe, when space is naturally restricted or when numerically superior.

Paradoxically, if the opponent is quick, you need to allow more space than when the attacker is moving slowly or stopped because the potential for acceleration is greatest at these speeds. When both the attacker and defender are moving quickly, acceleration isn't the problem but momentum is. You are vulnerable to rapid changes of direction and must assume a position to prevent this (e.g., sideways on).

The amount of space allowed the attacker will also depend on the direction the attacker is facing or moving. When the attacker is turned and facing their goalkeeper or dribbling away from your goal, you can safely be close. You can restrict space (pressure) when an attacker is alone or when you have a teammate's help (double-team). The amount of space given also varies with the area of the field. Generally, as the ball gets closer to the scoring area, allow less space.

When can you safely close the distance, and decrease the space? There are only certain times that it is safe. The common mistake of the inexperienced player is to rush uncontrolled at the attacker and hope to get the ball. Of course this works when the skill level of the attacker is low, but only proves to be embarrassing against better players. It is unfortunate that these aggressive, "pressure" tactics work at all. Players develop extremely bad habits that are difficult to change. A defender should decrease an attacker's space any time

Figure 133 Closing Down

One must be extremely cautious in approaching a skilled attacker, when they have control of the ball and their head up. The best procedure is often to do nothing and wait patiently. This is very disconcerting to the average paranoid attacker. When the attacker begins to move sideways it is then safe to decrease the space and apply more pressure.

they (attacker) are facing or moving in a direction other than toward goal (Fig. 133, pg. 118). Decreasing the space does not mean going for the ball. That is called "challenging" ("tackling" if the feet are used) and is discussed later.

Defensive Stance

"Thus, those skilled at making the enemy move do so by creating a situation to which he must conform." Sun Tzu

The individual defender plays an important role in a larger conflict — the battle between chaos and order. The attackers try to create maximum uncertainty and confusion among the defenders by using options, continuous movement, fakes and variation in the attack to increase defensive indecision. The defenders seek order and predictability, and to eliminate certain attacking options. This may be as simple as positioning to eliminate a pass to a supporting player or positioning to prevent movement in a certain direction. Be aware of an attacker's passing options and dribbling habits; use your stance to disrupt their plans.

The position the defender assumes with respect to the attacker will vary with the situation. When the attacker is in the middle of the field, and moving slowly or stopped, be between the ball and goal, well-balanced, feet shoulder-distance apart, knees bent, weight forward on the toes, and eyes on the ball (Table 23) (Fig. 134, pg. 120). Placing one foot slightly in front of the other allows faster starts. This basic defensive stance is very important — it is surprising how many beginning defenders are beaten simply because of a poor stance.

When the attacker is advancing the ball quickly, you will find it very difficult to run backward. Instead, turn to run comfortably, in a position facing the same direction as the attacker. When turned in this manner, assume a position off the attacker's shoulder, toward the middle of the field (Fig. 106, pg. 89). This allows you to run comfortably, change direction, watch the ball, and make a play for any loose balls. In addition, this position will encourage the attacker to move away from the middle of the field. This is called "jockeying" or "guiding". Defending in this manner is a good example of how you can use body position to control attackers and remove movement and passing options.

Although jockeying is most useful along the sidelines, it can be used in the center of the field when the attacker is still far from the goal. This stance is

---

Defensive Stance

- Eyes on ball
- Weight evenly distributed
- Weight forward on toes
- Feet shoulder distance apart
- Knees bent

Table 23

particularly useful on fastbreaks because the defender is turned to run with the attacker—as opposed to attempting to run backward.

Defenders are first taught to position themselves between the ball and the goal, rather than "jockeying", for good reason. In "jockeying" the defender is not between the ball and goal but is to one side of the attacker. This allows through passes and shots on goal. This technique is obviously not to be used when there are attacking players in the through position or when the ball is within shooting distance of the goal. This is why the technique is used most often on the sides of the field where the passes are permitted go square rather than toward goal.

Figure 134 Defensive Stance

The defender's stance will vary depending on their skill, the area of the field and whether or not the attacker is moving. The basic stance, with the defender stopped or moving slowly in the center of the field, is simple but important. The feet are shoulder-distance apart, the knees are bent and the weight forward on the toes. The eyes focus on the ball. The defender usually plays off a short distance. When both players are stopped or moving slowly with an intervening space, it is called a "neutral situation", because neither has an advantage.

Figure 135 Sideways-On

The classic defensive position is facing the attacker on a line between the ball and goal. However, there are certain disadvantages to this position. First, the defender cannot run backwards very well. Second, the attacker is given an option to go either right or left. Because of these drawbacks an alternate defensive position is sometimes used. In this stance, the defender faces in the same direction as the attacker and takes a position near one shoulder. The advantages are that the defender can run easily with the attacker and prevent movement to the middle. However, the defender cannot stop forward movement, forward passes or shots.

Use this technique with some discretion against attackers who are very fast. Because the guiding stance is to the side of the attacker, it invites a footrace. There is no obstacle between the attacker and the field ahead. Therefore, when faced with a faster opponent guiding is risky. Unfortunately, no matter how you choose to defend against a faster opponent there is great risk.

Figure 136 Preventing Wall Passes

Wall passes can be prevented in several ways. The most important thing is not to become a beatable defender. Beatable defenders are usually marking too closely or playing too aggressively. Another way to prevent wall passes is to sprint backwards if the player you are covering makes a square or through pass. This automatic movement, illustrated in these two photos, prevents the attacker from getting behind you to receive a return pass.

Figure 137 Preventing Wall Passes

Patience

"He who is prudent and lies in wait for an enemy who is not, will be victorious." Sun Tzu

Teaching patience is a great coaching challenge. Inexperienced defenders are uncomfortable waiting and make foolish attempts at getting the ball. This impatience decreases their chances of getting the ball. The defender that recklessly tries to get the ball is beaten. On the other hand, an impatient attacker often gives the patient defender the ball.

Preventing Wall Passes

The opportunity for wall passes is most frequently created by aggressive defending at the ball. The best prevention (Table 24) is to give the attacker a little space and be patient. This conservative style of defensive play prevents the attacker from passing, sprinting past you, and then getting a return ball. Many wall passes can be foiled and passes intercepted if the defender sprints backward a short distance every time the covered attacker makes a square pass (Fig. 136 & 137, pg. 121). This simple maneuver puts you neatly in the path of any return passes (Fig. 131 & 132, pg. 117).

Preventing Wall Passes
• Don't be a beatable defender
• Don't be too aggressive
• Don't get too close
• Don't stand when attacker is moving
• Automatically sprint backwards if the player you are marking makes a square or through pass

Table 24

Figure 138 Poke Tackle

This photo shows what is called a "poke" tackle. It is really a desperate attempt to spear the ball away from someone that is beating you. In the "hook" tackle the sliding defender is able to get the full foot in front of the ball. The ankle is flexed to temporarily grasp the ball, until the attacker invariably stumbles.

Tackling

To tackle is to use the feet in an attempt to take the ball from an opponent. The terms, "poke tackle," "sliding tackle," and "wedge tackle" refer to some of the techniques of winning the ball (Fig. 138, pg. 122) (Fig. 139 & 140, pg. 123). One of the first things to learn about tackling is that a missed tackle is much worse than no tackle. A missed tackle means a beaten

Figure 139 Slide Tackle

To tackle is to attempt to get the ball. Most frequently this is done with the feet. In physical conflicts over the ball, possession usually goes to the player with the largest, most well-planted surface behind the ball. A player successfully executing a blocking slide tackle, illustrated here, has a high probability of getting the ball. Unfortunately, if the tackle is mistimed the defender is on the ground, totally out of the play.

Figure 140 Slide Tackle

defender. There may not be time to recover, especially with the sliding tackle, because the defender is on the ground and out of play.

Perhaps more important than learning the technique of tackling, is learning when it is safe to tackle (Table 25). It is safe to tackle when the defender will have time to recover (as in the offensive end of the field), when the defenders outnumber attackers at the ball, and when absolutely certain of gaining possession. Be careful about tackling in neutral situations and when you are the last defender (Table 26). If you are the last defender and make an unsuccessful attempt at the ball, a goal could be scored (Fig. 141, pg. 125). Impulsive tackles in neutral situations are a primary cause of beaten defenders.

Timing is vitally important in tackling. The defender can safely get the ball any time the dribbler is too close to avoid the tackle. The critical distance, the "reaction distance", relates to human reaction time. Because of the delay due to reaction time, a player can move a certain distance before an opponent can respond. This distance is the "reaction distance". An attacking player that is moving quickly forward with the ball has a greater "reaction distance" — their speed means they will move farther before responding. Momentum and inattentiveness also increase the reaction distance. Any time players are closer together than the critical reaction distance, they cannot react quickly enough to counter an action by the other. Well-timed tackles are a result of an awareness of these factors — knowing precisely when an attacker can't respond to an attempt at the ball.

"His potential is that of a fully drawn crossbow; his timing, the release of the trigger." Sun Tzu

A tackle must be sudden. This means the attacker must be close, within the "reaction distance". For most speeds this means the attacker is one stride away. Any farther than this and the attacker will have time to evade the tackle.

The player that gets the ball in a tackle is the one that is the most firmly planted. This is why a bigger player has an advantage. A player should try to put their weight on the foot behind the ball. A sliding tackle works well because the defender's entire body is on the ground behind the ball. Just as there are times when a player should be cautious about tackling, there are times when tackling is more likely to be successful. The best time to attempt to get the ball is when a player is receiving it (Fig. 125, pg. 113). It is difficult for the attacker to concentrate on both an approaching ball and an approaching defender. Another tackling opportunity occurs when the attacker is looking away or at the ball.

Safe Times to Tackle
• In offensive third of field
• When attacker is isolated and outnumbered
• When probability of success is high
• When defender can touch ball first

Table 25

When Not to Tackle
• When you are the last defender
• When opponent is skilled, has their head up, and the ball under control
• When success is uncertain

Table 26

Figure 141 When Not to Tackle

Being aggressive involves risk. Hasty, ill-timed tackles do not succeed against good players in control of the ball. Another definite "no-no" is tackling when outnumbered. When outnumbered you should only tackle if you are absolutely confident of success. Otherwise, delay and wait for help. In this 3-vs.-1 the defender's tackle is simply avoided by an easy square pass.

A defensive feint will often cause an attacker to move the ball laterally, making the ball vulnerable. It also may force the attacker to watch the ball. An attacker watching the ball can't see open players for passes and can be more safely pressured by a defender.

Fast-moving attackers are more vulnerable to tackling because they take longer strides, change direction more slowly, and generally have less control. A slow-moving attacker takes shorter steps, responds more quickly, and therefore is less susceptible.

Perhaps the most common time to tackle is when the dribbler has lost control of the ball for a short time. The ball may have hit a rough spot on the field, been pushed too far forward or be too far back between the feet. For a brief instant, the defender can get to the ball first, poking it free (usually to one side) and establishing control. A defensive feint may sometimes cause one of these fleeting tackle opportunities.

Analyzing the Attacker

"Know the enemy and know yourself; in a hundred battles you will never be in peril." Sun Tzu

It is important for a defender to learn to analyze an attacker's preferred method of beating defenders (Table 27). Is it with sheer speed, is it with quick changes of direction, is it by stops and starts, is it by screening and turning? Most dribblers develop one or two favorite methods and use them repeatedly but the best dribblers are more flexible and use a variety of approaches. It also may be useful to know what they do in different dribbling situations. For example, how do they act in different offensive stances (facing, turned sideways, side-by-side, fully-turned)? How do they react to different defensive stances: playing off, sideways-on, double-teamed? Do they have difficulty handling any one of these (they may show this by passing)? Are they right-footed, and do they prefer dribbling in one direction over the other? Do they shoot only with one foot? How have they lost the ball before?

Knowing this information, defensive adjustments can be made. A fast attacker can be marked by a fast defender, or a second defender can always be nearby. A dribbler good at changing direction should be slowed and stopped (changing direction doesn't work as well when standing still). The defender also can try playing sideways-on — preventing the option of moving in one direction. A defender can overplay attackers that screen and turn, blocking the direction they prefer to turn. Double-teaming also works — bringing a second defender from their blind side. These are just some examples of the common-sense approaches to individual defensive problems.

Double-Teaming

Two defenders working together have a greater probability of getting the ball from an attacker. Double-team where it is difficult for attackers to support (in the corners, by the sidelines), when there is limited support (no square or through passing options), when the attacker is greatly outnumbered, and in front of the goal. It may be productive to double-team any time a defender forces an attacker to watch the ball (Fig. 97, pg. 83).

To effectively double-team, two defenders must communicate and work together. The first sets up the attacker so the second can get the ball. The first defender may take up a position to force the attacker to move toward the second defender with the ball exposed, or the first defender can force the attacker to watch the ball and not see the approach of the second defender. A third method is for the first defender to tackle suddenly forcing the attacker to kick the ball far to one side — closer to the second defender. This technique works especially well against fast-approaching attackers.

Double-teaming is not without its risks. If the defenders are too close, a fast attacker can go by both. If they are too far apart, they can be beaten separately by an attacker with good ball control. An attacker can slip the ball between two side-by-side defenders, beating them to it or being fouled in the process.

Attacker Analysis, Consider:
• Preferred method of beating defenders
• Speed
• Cuts
• Fakes
• Other move
• Preferred direction of movement
• Dominant foot & shooting foot
• Preferred area of field (center, flanks)
• Preferred stance with respect to defender
• How have they lost ball before?

Table 27

Figure 142 Double-Teaming

Double-teaming the player with the ball increases the probability that the defense will get the ball. However, it is not without risk. When two defenders are concentrating on one attacker, there is another attacker open somewhere. Also, if two defenders are beaten the consequences are often greater. For these reasons, double-teaming is often restricted to safe areas (sidelines, corners), to important areas (goal area) or important circumstances (time's running out and we gotta get the ball back). The ultimate aggressive policy is to double-team any time an attacker is forced to be a ball watcher. Double-teaming is harder in the middle, as in this photo.

Delaying Techniques

"He who knows when he can fight and when he cannot will be victorious." Sun Tzu

Delaying techniques give the defense time to get back and organized after turnovers. They are especially important on fastbreaks and when outnumbered. There are two methods of delay — high pressure and low pressure.

With high pressure, the defender gets close and forces the attacker to watch the ball and spend time struggling to keep possession. The attacker, with their head down, is unable to see passing opportunities. Use this type of delay when you are close to an attacker who is getting the ball on a turnover. Get close before the attacker gets their head up or the opportunity will be lost.

If the attacker has time to control the ball and look up, delay by encouraging them to dribble instead of pass. In these circumstances, play loosely, covering angles for through passes or potential pass recipients. Because dribbling is the slowest means of advancing the ball, discouraging passing and encouraging dribbling gives your teammates more time to get back and organize.

The Fastbreaking Attacker

I t happens! Your team finishes an attack and the opposing goalie launches an immediate counterattack. You are the only defender between the ball and the goal (Fig. 143 to 145, pg. 129). While avoiding being beaten, you would like to delay the attack, force the attack away from goal, and then prevent a shot or centering pass (Table 28). To do this, follow these steps: Delay the attack by offering loose resistance at the ball (low pressure), causing the attacker to dribble slower and with control. Use body position or "jockeying" to encourage movement away from the center. When the attacker is within shooting distance, position between the ball and goal to prevent shots. If the ball has been forced to the outside, your priority is to prevent passes to any open attackers in the center. Assist in blocking shots only when they are from a dangerous angle, and always assume a position that will prevent the centering pass. Hopefully, by now, your teammates will have arrived to help.

Outnumbered!

"If weaker numerically, be capable of withdrawing." Sun Tzu

H ow do you handle the situation where there are two or three attackers facing you—the lone defender (Fig. 146 to 148, pg. 130)? You would like to delay the attack, force the play from the middle, and prevent a successful shot on goal (Table 28). Delay the attack by either pressuring at the ball or giving space. Body positioning will encourage movement of the ball away from the middle of the field. If the ball is passed to the outside of the field or dribbled away from the middle, stay in the center. This will discourage movement back toward the best scoring area. As the ball approaches the goal and becomes a scoring threat, move toward it. The goalie can easily handle most shots coming from the sides, because of the poor shooting angles. The defender's role is to prevent movement or passing toward the middle of the field and to help block shots to the far post. The defender should approach the ball at an angle that discourages centering passes. If the ball is in the middle, the defender must be in position to prevent a shot. This may not be easy with two free attackers, so delaying is perhaps the most important element.

Other players should be sprinting back, trying to get between the ball and the goal ("goal-side"). In emergencies such as this, the true value of positions is most evident — they are totally disregarded. Although players making "recovery runs" make a bee-line for the penalty spot to participate in the defense, it

Fastbreak or Outnumbered
• Delay
• Don't be beaten
• Force play to the outside
• Protect the center, prevent movement and passing to the center
• Approach ball when scoring threat is high but at an angle to prevent centering pass

Table 28

Figure 143 Fastbreak Goof-Up

On a fastbreak you would like to delay, force the attack from the middle, and keep the ball from the best scoring area. The defender in this two-on-one failed on two counts. He didn't do a very good job of delaying and he left the middle too early. His position at the ball did not prevent a pass to the middle. He may not have seen the player running up the middle. If that is the case, he is also guilty of ball-watching. You have to constantly check the space behind you. The attackers scored.

Figure 144 Fastbreak Goof-Up

On offense, the objective in a 2-on-1 situation is to get the ball to an open attacker in the middle. If, as in this case, the defender comes out from the middle too early the job is relatively easy. The player dribbling down the outside of the field need only pass to their teammate in the middle. If the defender is much smarter and stays in the middle then the player with the ball should dribble at an angle across the field toward the far corner. The other attacking player should ..

Figure 145 Fastbreak Goof-Up

wait until they have just passed the middle, then run behind them toward the opposite corner of the field. This crossing movement confuses the defenders and goalie. It draws the defense out of position and creates a good opportunity for the second attacker to take a drop pass or back-heel pass and shoot into the open net on the far side of the goal. A similar crossing movement is also useful in 2-on-2 fastbreaks.

Figure 146 Outnumbered

The defender in this 3-vs-1 became impatient and forced the play. He could have delayed longer. By staying in the middle he forced play to outside attackers with poor shooting angles. Fortunately, the defender had teammates that hustle. One of them came all the way back and intercepted the ball. Only when the ball is in the back of the net is it too late to hustle back and help.

Figure 147 Outnumbered

Figure 148 Outnumbered

isn't always necessary to "recover" all the way back. In fact, the first defenders usually just get goal-side and either support the first defender or help cover opponents and space away from the ball.

Chapter 6

Organizing the Defense

"A confused army leads to another's victory." Sun Tzu

Summary: Successful defense requires good individual defending, organization and numerical superiority. Individual skill is the foundation of good defense. Defenders marking at the ball or covering players away from the ball must not be beaten. Organization of markings begins at the ball and proceeds logically, based on an assessment of the threat. The team's general defensive strategy influences the organization of these markings. By denying space, the defense achieves the broad defensive objectives of preventing goals and regaining possession of the ball.

Principles of Good Defense

The principles of good defense are these: 1) defend well individually, 2) outnumber the attackers between the ball and goal, and 3) organize well and quickly.

Good Individual Defense

Good individual defending, discussed in the previous chapter, is the cornerstone of good team defense. The foundation of the entire defense is the individual defender. With good defenders the defense can play with aggressive confidence. With weak defenders the defense is timid, loose and often disorganized.

Creating Superior Numbers

Although outnumbering an opponent doesn't guarantee defensive success, it helps. The defense usually employs tactics that ensure more defenders than attackers between the ball and goal. With superior numbers there is greater safety for the defense and less time and space for the attacking players (more pressure).

The methods of producing this superiority include: 1) making sure everyone defends, 2) teaching the process of "recovery" (Fig. 158, pg. 143) on turnovers, 3) having all marking defenders try to stay "goal-side" (Fig. 161, pg. 145), and 4) concentrating in greater numbers when approaching the goal.

Figure 149 Numerical Superiority

The quest for numerical superiority by the defense may have unfortunate consequences. Unproductive and unpredictable bunches are the usual result. The quest for numerical superiority near this throw-in has resulted in a poorly protected goal area. Fortunately for the defense, the attacking team is poorly positioned to use the advantage.

Numerical Superiority

Although there are limits, having superior numbers on offense or defense is generally advantageous. For defense, it is true that "There is safety in numbers". Additional numbers not only mean that each attacker will be covered but there will be additional defenders that can provide pressure at the ball, double-cover threatening opponents or provide coverage for beaten teammates.

Since both sides have 11 players, superior numbers can be created only temporarily in selective areas. The area chosen by the defense is between the ball and the goal being defended. Often the defense chooses an even more restricted space — the area immediately in front of the goal (the "vital space"). Creating numerical superiority in areas away from goal weakens the defense in the important area in front of goal (Fig. 149, pg. 133).

To achieve numerical superiority requires a cooperative team effort. On turnovers everyone must help, quickly moving to a position between the ball and

Figure 150 Using the Offsides Rule

The defending team on this free kick, by playing in a line, is using the offsides rule to restrict the movements of the attacking players. This is a fairly safe tactic this close to goal, because the goalkeeper can cover the space created behind the defense quite well. Farther from goal the risk is greater.

Space & Defense

To prevent goals and regain possession of the ball, the defense restricts attacking space (creates pressure). Space can be restricted by marking individual attackers or covering areas. These methods correspond to defensive systems of "man-on-man" (Fig. 157, pg. 142) coverage and "zone" coverage (Fig. 156, pg. 141). Neither of these systems is perfect. Passes and runs into space beat defenders that concentrate solely on tight individual markings. When the focus is entirely on covering large spaces, individual attackers have greater freedom and small but useful amounts of space. A compromise between these two theoretical approaches often is the best approach.

In marking players, the same conflict exists between protecting space and covering the individual attacker. When a defender marks too tightly, the attacker can often make a surprise run and beat the defender into space (Fig. 57, pg. 48). If the defender is covering too loosely a pass can be made to the covered player's feet. Only by knowing the abilities of the opponents can a defender achieve a successful compromise.

goal. This not only requires fitness, but often an attitude adjustment by certain players that only like to attack. Successful defense is a team effort.

Compactness

"If I concentrate while he divides, I can use my entire strength to attack a fraction of his." Sun Tzu

Defensive compactness magnifies the effect of superior numbers. Channeling the defenders into a small area creates compactness. The attacking players can be forced to develop their attack within this confined space by defensive use of the offsides rule or by choosing a space close to goal, where the attackers must inevitably come.

Drawing together near the ball and in the goal area is a natural defensive impulse — it makes the defense more efficient. "Funnelling" refers to the process of defenders clustering together as the attackers approaches goal. Funnelling assures a compact defense in which the attackers have less space, and smaller lanes for through passes. Defenders can behave more aggressively with less risk because others are nearby to provide assistance. Forcing the attack to develop within the compact defense increases the probability of defensive success.

There are two different methods of encouraging these circumstances. One method is to use the offsides rule (Fig. 150, pg. 134). The last line of defenders plays in a line across the field. No attacker can cross that line unless they have the ball or are pursuing the ball. This forces the attackers to develop their attack in the somewhat restricted space in front of the defense. The second method is to set up the compact defense close to goal, an area to which the attackers must eventually come if they want to score. Often, both methods are used simultaneously in the goal area.

Good Organization

Good organization is a product of knowledge (of oneself and one's opponent), leadership, communication and commonly understood team policies. To be successful an organizational system requires a team of disciplined, responsible individuals (Table 21, pg. 102).

The Organizational Process

The organization of defenders must be rapid and orderly. A lack of organization leads to confusion, open attackers, and goals. Team strategy is an important element of organization. Without a commonly understood team policy, organization on the field will be difficult as each player pursues their interpretation of what is best for the team. The specific elements of team tactics that must be decided include: area of organized resistance and how it may vary under different circumstances, organization of markings (e.g., true individual markings vs. territories), how markings may vary (with different areas of the field, different attackers, different game situations), how aggressive to be, how support is to be provided and whether to use offsides tactics (Table 29, pg. 137). The organized team also must know how it will defend against offensive set plays.

Defensive organization requires field vision, individual commitment, leadership and communication. In all situations, except when outnumbered, the starting point for defense is marking at the ball (Fig. 151, pg. 136). This must be done quickly after a turnover and each time the opponents pass the ball. Until this crucial commitment is made, the defense cannot organize and other players will be uncertain about their roles. If the closest player to the ball is hesi-

Figure 151 Communication
Communication is probably more important to defense than offense because organization is so important and so dependent on communication. Both talking and pointing are important. This photo illustrates the process. The essential first step in the organization process is a verbal commitment by the closest defender to the ball to mark at the ball. This should be announced to rest of the team ("Ball!") so they can get on with covering other players. It is surprising how frequently this is a problem — no one wants the responsibility. It is a shirking of duty that frequently leads to goals being scored. An analogous situation on offense is when no one wants the responsibility of shooting (and maybe missing), so the ball is passed and the scoring opportunity (and maybe the game) is lost.

Team Factors in Organization

- Area of first defensive resistance

- Defense on turnovers with variations in different areas

- Organization of markings
  - Individual
  - Zone
  - Hybrid

- Variations in markings
  - Field area
  - Specific attacking players
  - Game situations

- Aggression level

- Method of support

- Use of offsides rule?

Table 29

tant the team leader or another player should direct. Covering the ball is the crucial first step in defensive organization.

Defensive Support

The need to be concerned with covering for teammates who may be beaten makes coverage difficult. Providing this backup coverage is called "defensive support". In practical terms, there must be at least one other defender closer to the goal than the defender at the ball. The closest defender "plays at an angle" behind the defender at the ball. This second defender plays close to a line between the ball and the goal (Fig. 152, pg. 137). The exact position is usually a compromise that allows partial coverage of any through or square attacking player (Fig. 165, pg. 148). The distance of the supporting defender will depend on the defensive objective (closer when double-teaming to win the ball), the area of the field (closer in the goal area), whether the attacker is moving (looser) and whether there are supporting attackers (looser). The supporting defender would like to be positioned to intercept balls played past the first defender in attempts to dribble to goal.

A special name, "the sweeper", has been created for a defensive player whose primary defensive function is to act as a "safety", supporting the last line of defenders (Fig. 152 & 157 pg. 137 & 142). The sweeper may support directly at the ball, in the role of the "second" defender, or else cover space behind the defense. Support is always more important to the last line of defenders because players farther upfield always have teammates behind them. Poor support in the last line of defense is a primary cause of goals.

Figure 152 Defensive Support

On defense, as on offense, support is an important principle. An appropriate synonym for "support" is "to help". Helping on defense means being behind the defender at the ball to cover should they be beaten. There are several ways of providing this support. A nearby defender can position behind the ball to provide this coverage, but the last line of defenders is often supported by a special player — the sweeper. This photo shows the sweeper at work. His job description includes supporting at the ball, sweeping up passes behind the defense, and covering other unmarked players that might threaten.

Covering the Players Close to the Ball

After covering the player with the ball, the coverage follows a simple, logical process based on first covering those players that represent the greatest threat to score (Fig. 153 & 154, pg. 139). This means that defenders must quickly check the scoring area (the "vital space") and the space behind them, making sure there are no unmarked players (ball watching is a common, serious defensive error (Fig. 110, pg. 94). Next, they should cover the players around the ball

After the ball, the defense should cover the through players because they are closer to goal. Cover the square players next, but ignore the back players unless they are a threat to score. Normal defensive position is between the player being marked and the goal. How tightly they are marked depends on the direction the attacker is facing, their speed, skill, closeness to goal, closeness to the ball, and the need to cover for nearby defenders (Table 30). Coverage is gen-

Variables in Markings
• Relative speed & fitness (attacker vs. defender)
• Relative skill (attacker vs. defender)
• Area of field
• Direction facing
• Distance from ball
• Presence of nearby attackers
• Team strategy
• Score

Table 30

Figure 153 Covering Order

This photo shows the field just after a turnover. Most of the defenders are hastily recovering to the goal area. This is understandable because the space be- hind the defense is about to be invaded. This could have been prevented if someone had taken responsibility and quickly marked at the ball.

First, Second and Third Defenders

Some coaches refer to a defending player away from the ball in a figurative way as "the third defender." The first defender marks the ball and provides "pressure." The second defender supports the first and "covers." The role of the third defender is to cover the space behind the defense away from the ball, to provide "balance."

erally tighter closer to the ball, closer to goal, when the attacker is slow or unskilled, when the attacker is turned and when the defender at the ball is good. The coverage will be a unique reflection of the defender's abilities relative to the opposing attacker.

"Know the enemy and know yourself; in a hundred battles you will never be in peril." Sun Tzu

Generally, a defender shouldn't cover square players too closely (Fig. 155, pg. 140). Marking a square player too tightly may have several consequences. First, defenders are easier to beat — with no time to evaluate and respond to sudden bursts of speed or changes of direction by the attacker. Second, by covering tightly a defender increases the amount of space closer to goal, making penetrating passes behind them easier. Third, when a defender is too close they may be too far away or up-field to back up (support) the defender at the

Figure 154 Covering Order

A defender has just been beaten and the attacker is centering the ball. Instead of centering the ball immediately, this player should have moved along the end line toward goal. This threat would have drawn out the goalie, brought the central defender (near the six yard line) to the ball (creating more space in the middle) and created an excellent scoring opportunity for #4. As it is, the defense is well-situated in the center where the greatest scoring threat exists. Cover the scoring area first!

ball. For these reasons, defenders should give the square attackers some space. Doing this allows an increased number of square passes, but, since square passes do not advance the ball toward goal, they are not of great concern.

Offensive players positioned behind the ball are usually only covered when they represent a threat to score. In general, the defense concentrates between the ball and the goal, allowing some square and back passes. The defense allows offensive possession in return for a diminished scoring threat. This convenient arrangement changes when the defending team needs to score.

Coverage Away From the Ball

Zone Defense

In the traditional zone system, defenders cover players or space in areas or zones (Fig. 156, pg. 141) corresponding to their position in the team's formation. The location of these areas will vary with the defensive tactics. For example, with a retreating defense the areas are close together near the scoring area. In its most common form, defenders mark players around the ball and close to goal individually, while covering spaces in areas farther from the ball. An attacking player is a defender's responsibility only when they are in that defender's zone. When the attacker leaves that zone, they become the responsibility of another defender.

Fitness and Team Defense

When fatigued, players are unable to get back quickly on defense. Concentration and discipline also lag. Late in a match it often becomes difficult to maintain the tactics that have created a secure, numerically superior defense. This is one reason that more goals are scored in the final fifteen minutes of a game.

Figure 155 Bad Coverage?

The defender (#20) covering the square player is certainly giving generous amounts of space. Many inexperienced players would consider this bad defense. It isn't. The square player is no direct threat. Defender #20 is improving the defense by partially covering the angle for a penetrating pass and he is better situated to assist if one is made. Imagine how big the lane for a through pass would be if he moved forward 15 feet!

Zone defense has advantages and disadvantages. It is easy to achieve a compact defense by concentrating defenders closer to goal. The system is not as vulnerable to attacking movements designed to create space. Defenders are freer to watch and react to the ball, can cover spaces away from the ball more easily and are less likely to be beaten because markings are usually looser. Transitions between offense and defense are quicker in "zone" defenses. On the other hand, zones can be overloaded (too many attackers for the defenders in the area to cover) and attackers often have more space in the zone defensive system.

Individual Markings

The classic alternative to the zone defense is a system of individual markings, usually called a "man-on-man" defense (Fig. 157, pg. 142). In this system,

Figure 156 Zone Defense

This photo shows a classic bunch. The offense can go nowhere. The defense is also arrayed in a loose "zone" defense. Defenders are covering areas, not individuals. As a result, nearby attackers have small amounts of space, but nothing tremendously useful. Unfortunately, the attackers are not able to use the huge space on the far side.

defenders stick to their markings, following their attacker everywhere until possession is regained.

Although individual markings have a great theoretical advantage (totally removing each attacker's space), few teams can successfully use the system with 11 player teams (the system is easier with smaller sides). This system requires superior organization, fitness, concentration, discipline, and one-on-one skill. Successful organization requires good player vision, leadership and good communication. Because of the organizational difficulties, teams that are young or less experienced should avoid this defense.

Perhaps the greatest weakness of this defense is the lack of defensive support. Someone is needed to cover for beaten defenders and help protect the space behind the defense. Teammates can abandon their coverage to back up a teammate but this is usually awkward and confusing. Also, there just may not be a teammate in a position to help.

Figure 157 Individual Markings

The advantages of individual markings are well-illustrated in this photo. No attacker has usable space. The success of the offense is entirely dependent on its ability to win one-on-ones. However, the sweeper, seen behind the defense, provides additional safety against this eventuality. If the offense is static and stuck in a rigid formation, this is exactly the situation that often results. The principle method of disrupting the marking system (other than beating defenders) is free, creative (confusing) movement.

A system of individual markings has other drawbacks. Defenders become so intent on their markings that they forget to also watch the ball, often missing opportunities to intercept passes. Defenders preoccupied with their defensive markings may be reluctant contributors to the team's offense. For the same reason, transitions between defense and offense may be slow.

Compactness is more difficult to achieve with individual markings, as the positions of the defenders are largely controlled by the attacking team. This can be partly overcome by two strategies — marking attackers in positions behind the ball from a goal-side position and using loose or "sagging" coverage of square players. The degree to which these strategies are implemented is a team tactical decision that is largely determined by the strength of the opponent.

Figure 158 Recovery

To "recover" is to move to a defensive position between the ball and the goal being defended. A player recovers after any turnover or when beaten. The exact place to which a defender recovers will depend on an assessment of the particular situation at the time of the turnover. In general, the closest defender to the ball will position goal-side and pressure at the ball. The second defender will support the first. Third and successive defenders will first cover less threatening attackers and then try to protect the space behind the defense. If in doubt a defender can always move to the "universal recovery site" — the penalty spot.

Variations in the individual marking system that help overcome its shortcomings include use of a sweeper (Fig. 157, pg. 142) and selective individual markings. Use of the sweeper helps overcome the principle problems — beaten defenders, unmarked attackers and coverage of the space behind the defense. Using individual markings selectively against certain individuals or within certain areas retains the advantages of this system (pressure) while helping to minimize some weaknesses.

In "total football", a system of individual markings is more easily employed. While fitness and individual mismatches will always be a problem, a "total football" system doesn't have as many organizational problems, or conflicts between following an attacker and "playing one's position". Despite the many difficulties, a system of individual markings remains the defensive ideal.

Applications

2-on-2

"Generally, management of many is the same as management of few. It is a matter of organization." Sun Tzu

Two-on-two is a defensive model with useful but simplified tactical problems. Team tactics and organizational elements are present, but the game is especially suited for studying the problems of support and marking away from the ball. The critical role played by the defender at the ball and the implications for team defense are never more obvious than in the two-on-two.

Defensive strategy in the two-on-two does not include deciding how many players will participate in the defense — to avoid disaster everyone must defend. The defensive team should decide what its general defensive strategy will be. Will pressure be used to create turnovers in the offensive end (Fig. 159, pg. 145) or will the defense set up close to goal (Fig. 160, pg. 145) and launch quick counterattacks? Will a zone defense or individual markings be used?

Generally, the most successful strategy in two-on-two is to use individual markings, to retreat and set up the defense close to the goal, to score by quick counterattacks, and to selectively pressure a weaker opponent to create turnovers. The second defender creates numerical superiority between the ball and goal by always staying goal-side. Even with the second attacker positioned or

What to Do When Beaten

What you will do if the opponent you are marking gets past you will depend on the reaction of teammates and how quickly you can recover. If you are fast, you can get back into a position between the attacker and goal. If an attacker dribbles around you and then a teammate moves to cover, you should hustle back to a position between your teammate and goal. That is, you "recover" to a supporting position. Your exact position will depend somewhat upon the threat posed by other attackers and whether any of your teammates are providing assistance. If beaten by a pass to someone you have been covering away from the ball, the situation is similar — hustle to a recovery position.

Figure 159 Non-Retreating Defense

Team tactics apply in 2-on-2. The defending team must decide whether to pressure over the entire length of the field or to retreat and set up near goal. In this figure they have decided to pressure in the offensive half. These pressure tactics sometimes result in easy goals — for both teams. The problem is the large space behind the defense. This space gives the attacking team an advantage if they have the tools to use it.

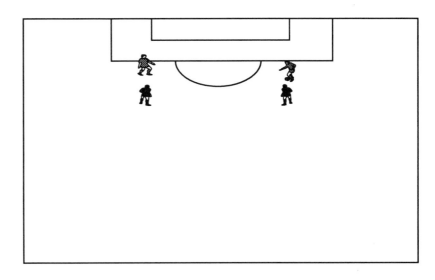

Figure 160 Retreating Defense

The retreating defense has many advantages. Many of these are apparent in the 2-on-2. The closer the defense sets up to goal, the smaller the space the offense has to work with. The offense can't get behind the defense because there is little room. The defenders are close together, allowing better teamwork. Other advantages are more apparent with bigger teams — time to get organized and better vision of the developing attack.

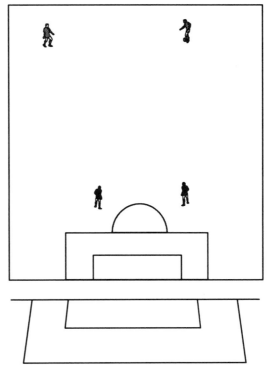

Figure 161 Staying Goal-Side

The second defender normally stays goalside, even when the attacker is behind the ball. Only under exceptional circumstances (team behind in the closing minutes) would the second defender cover the second attacker standing behind the ball. The second defender usually "tracks" the movements of the second attacker from a goal-side position. In 2-on-2 the primary reason for this policy is the need to back up the defender at the ball. With larger teams, this goalside position allows greater protection against penetrating passes.

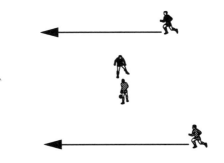

Figure 162 Defender at Ball is a Wimp

With the ball in the center and a mismatched defender at the ball, the second defender must assume a position to cover should the first defender be beaten. The exact position of the second defender will depend on their speed, what the probability of the first defender being beaten is (wimp factor), and how much of a threat the second attacker is. If the defender at the ball is really weak, position 1 is the best position. Position 2 is the normal position, assuming everyone is about equal in ability.

Figure 163 Sideline Menace

This photo partially illustrates the overwhelming importance of the center. No matter how strong the threat on the outside, the defense will be greatly influenced by the threat in the center (the scoring area). Unless the center attacker is totally incompetent, the defense must assure adequate coverage. At a distance from goal, this defender's position is a good compromise between support and covering the central threat. Closer to goal, the second defender would have to mark the central attacker more closely.

Figure 164 Defending With Mr. Right

With Mr. Invulnerable at the ball (first defender), your position (the second defender) depends on your abilities. If you are God's gift to defense, you may mark tightly (position 1). If the attacker is faster, position 2 is better. Generally, position 2 is preferred because Mr. Invulnerable is probably like the rest of us — prone to an occasional mistake. Incidentally, position 1 is better against a slower but very clever attacker. You can prevent passes to their feet.

Intercepting Passes

Learning to intercept more passes is difficult. If the defender marks too tightly passes are discouraged (which is OK), or worse, made to the space behind the covering defender. By offering space and then quickly removing it immediately before a pass, a good defender can often lure the player with the ball into making a pass that will be intercepted. By watching the eyes of the player with the ball, defenders can often anticipate and intercept more passes. To keep from being beaten yet intercept passes, the defender must assume a position with both the player being covered and the ball in view.

moving behind the ball, the second defender stays goal-side (Fig. 161, pg. 145).

The simple phrase, "I've got the ball" or more simply "Ball!", usually marks the beginning of defensive organization. On opposing goal kicks the defensive team may retreat to midfield (if that is their strategy) and wait before making any commitment. On sudden midfield turnovers the strategy is to stay in the center, delay and play loosely between and in front of the attackers, trading space for time — hoping your teammate will hustle back to help.

Two-on-two tests a defender's knowledge of the variables involved in marking attacking players away from the ball. The defender must balance the need to support the defender at the ball, the need to intercept direct passes, and the need to prevent passes to the space behind the defense. Backing up the teammate at the ball has a priority that will vary with the position of the ball on the field (Fig. 66, pg. 58). If there is a possibility that the defender at the ball may be beaten (Fig. 162, pg. 146), the second defender must be nearby and closer to goal. If this is not a risk, the second defender can concentrate more fully on marking the second attacker (Fig. 164, pg. 146). The considerations then become the second attacker's speed and the ability of the attacking team to work together to complete a pass behind the defense. With a fast attacking player, the defender must allow more space, in effect getting a head-start in any race for the ball. Even if the attacking player is very fast, there may be little risk if the attacking team cannot complete an accurate, well-timed pass.

Switching and combination plays are common in two-on-two. When the opponents switch or do a takeover, the least confusing thing for the defenders to do is to maintain their individual markings. If the opposing team can complete wall passes the defending team must be cautious about being too aggressive or marking too tightly at the ball.

5-on-5

With more players involved, the 5-on-5 introduces a greater degree of defensive complexity. It becomes more difficult to organize quickly and the presence of one or more through players affects defensive support and markings.

It is essential that all five players participate in defense. Although a team may decide to apply full-court pressure against a weaker team, a retreating type defense is usually more successful in small-sided games. The defending team applies pressure in the offensive third of the field after turnovers, even when using the retreating defense. However, the team retreats and delays when it becomes clear that the other team will successfully work the ball out of its end. Defense normally begins at midfield on goal kicks. With five players, a system of individual markings is less confusing than trying to play some form of zone defense based on positions. The defenders covering the through players are usually adequately positioned to support the defender at the ball. When the ball is at the last line of defenders, a nearby defender must assume a position that provides support. The considerations in these circumstances are similar to 2-on-2.

Coverage of through players is generally tight, dictated by the speed and the passing ability of the opponents. A defending player will be responsible for an attacker in a back position, but the defender will stay goal-side tracking or shadowing their movements while helping to contribute to the defense closer to goal (Fig. 165, pg. 148). As the goal is approached, the through players are covered more tightly and defenders farther away from goal funnel toward goal — creating a compact defense.

11-on-11

In 11-on-11, the defending team must decide whether organized resistance (pressure) is to be applied over the entire field, beginning at midfield or beginning in the defensive third (Table 29). How will that organization be affected by turnovers in different areas of the field? Should players away from the ball cover space or use a system of individual markings? Will the markings be based on "the formation" or will coverage be based on positions at the time of a turnover? Will a covering defender follow an attacker anywhere or just when in their territory? Should marking defenders always try to stay goal-side?

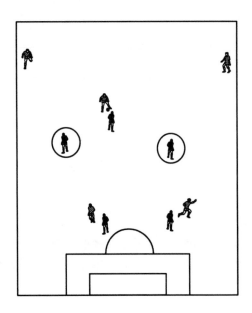

Figure 165 5-on-5

In 5-on-5, individual markings are natural. The through players are tightly covered. Additional coverage of through passing lanes is provided by sagging the defenders covering square. They stay in a goal-side position that allows them to support the defender at the ball, block through passing lanes, and temporarily double-team if necessary or advantageous.

Should defenders away from the ball sag to protect the spaces closer to goal? Will the last line of defenders use the offsides rule and play in a line? Will a sweeper provide coverage or how will support be provided? With eleven players defensive organization is complex. The following paragraphs are one possible approach to defense for a team with a sweeper and nine others playing "total football".

When the attack begins with a goal kick, the defending team waits near the midfield line. This encourages the opponents to play the ball short and to work the ball through all eleven defenders. (If the team plays up and pressures, a long goal kick can bypass two thirds of the defenders.)

However, on turnovers in the offensive third, the team applies pressure in the hopes of regaining possession. If the opponents look like they will break out (work the ball to a player with lots of space or else to the goalkeeper) the

Figure 166 Midfield Turnover

The principles of defense on turnovers in the middle and defensive thirds of the field are similar. The general principles are: organize, delay, force the attack from the middle, prevent passes behind the defense, don't get beaten, and everyone hustle back. These processes are at work in the photo. Players are recovering to goal-side positions. The pointing finger indicates some organization. A commitment is being made to the ball, with additional pressure on the way.

defense delays and retreats. On turnovers in the midfield and in the defensive third, the principles are to delay and for everyone to hustle to a goal-side position.

"Total football" uses individual markings. When the team loses possession, defenders mark the closest, most threatening attacker. At the time of a turnover a defender checks the field, assesses the situation, and usually marks the greatest threat they can. Communication between defenders is essential to organize the defense rapidly. The sweeper is particularly critical in the organizing effort — using their vantage point to assess the greatest threats and direct the coverage. The defenders will stick with their markings (no matter where they wander) until the team regains possession. Defenders away from the ball will sag to help cover space closer to goal — while still keeping track of their individual. Defenders marking attacking players behind the ball will stay goal-side, loosely following their roamings, covering tightly only if they become a scoring threat. These goal-side tactics create a surplus of defenders close to goal that allow additional pressure to be applied at the ball. Several defenders responsible for back-supporting attackers eventually abandon the goal-side bias (depending on the threat) when the attack approaches goal. They seek space where they can serve as outlets for launching counterattacks. The defense uses the offsides rule to advantage when the ball is within 18 yards of goal. The defense plays in a line across the field beginning at the edge of the penalty area. This line will only move toward goal to keep up with the advancing ball. When the ball retreats from goal the defense pushes forward, forcing all attackers away from goal. This tactic helps limit the attacking movements, creating confusion and frustration. The goalkeeper is close enough to support and scoop up any balls passed to the small space behind the defense.

Defense After Midfield Turnovers

Frequently, a team loses the ball unexpectedly. The principles of defending on turnovers (Fig. 166, pg. 149) are similar to situations where the defense is temporarily outnumbered. These principles are:

A. Assess. Look around, check the space closer to goal. Decide which players are the greatest threats.

B. Organize. This process begins with the closest defender providing coverage at the ball.

C. Delay. The best strategy is to get close and pressure before they get their head up. If the attacker has time and space to get turned and get their head up, looser coverage to encourage dribbling is the best method of delay.

D. Force the attack away from the middle. The defender at the ball uses body positioning to force the ball away from the dangerous central area of the field. When outnumbered cover the center first.

E. Don't get beaten. A beaten defender in these situations greatly compromises an already tenuous defense.

F. "Everyone hustle back!" Everyone must come back quickly so the whole defense can organize and proceed normally. The first defenders usually assume the functions of the 1st, 2nd and 3rd defenders as discussed earlier. Other defenders recover to an area between the ball and goal.

Photo by Phil Stephens

Chapter 7

Defensive Team Tactics

"Against those skilled in attack, an enemy does not know where to defend; against the experts in defense the enemy does not know where to attack." Sun Tzu

"To become invincible depends on you, the enemy's fate is his own..." Sun Tzu

Summary: In the normal developing defense (starting from an opponent's goal-kick) there are two types of team defense — full-field pressure and a retreating defense. These both have advantages and disadvantages. Full-field pressure is more common in amateur soccer because opponents do not have the skill or tactical expertise to overcome pressure.

Factors in team defense include characteristics of the opponent's team, game conditions, and characteristics of the defending team. Effective team defensive strategies must consider the interplay of all these elements.

Approaches to Team Defense

Full-Field Pressure

The defenses in soccer are comparable to those of basketball. An important consideration is where defensive resistance begins. Pressure can start in the offensive end (full-field), the middle or in the defensive end (retreating defense) of the field. There are advantages and disadvantages to each defense. With full-field pressure (Fig. 167, pg. 154) there is an increased chance of getting the ball by creating a turnover. The trade-off is an increased risk of giving up easy goals if the opponent breaks out.

Advantages of Retreating Defense
• Time to organize
• More compact defense
• No space behind defense for attackers to penetrate
• Greaters defensive numbers
• Attack must develop in front of defense (in full view)
• Opportunity for quick counter-attacks

Table 31

The characteristics of a full-field pressure-type defense are tight individual markings in the offensive third, aggressive individual defensive play, and frequently, use of the offsides rule to confine the opponents.

The full-field pressure type defense is routine in amateur soccer. This defense is also common when a team is trailing late in the match. The purpose under these conditions is to get the ball back quickly to make up the score difference. It is effective because teams don't have the skills or tactical sophistication necessary to overcome pressure. These same deficiencies mean they can not exploit the opportunities created by these defensive tactics. Full-field pressure is probably more successful in soccer than basketball (full-court pressure) because the offensive task is more difficult and complex due to the greater number of players.

Retreating Defense

"Knowing the place and time of the coming battle, we may concentrate from the greatest distances to fight." Sun Tzu

"The enemy will be tired and you will be rested if you lure him to you." Sun Tzu

In soccer, as in war, there are some positions that are more easily defended than others. For this reason, most professional teams retreat and organize their defense closer to goal (Table 31, Fig. 167). By retreating, the team gains time to organize. Like the Russians in World War II, territory is exchanged for time. With the time gained, the defense can gather strength and organize. Organization and resistance begin at midfield and increase as the defense assembles in front of goal. Two of the more common variations involve use of individual markings around the penalty area and use of the offsides rule near the 18 yard line.

The retreating defense has significant advantages. The attack must develop in front of the defense, giving the defenders a good view. There is no space behind the defense to be exploited by through passes or by beating defenders. This defense also creates opportunities for quick counterattacks. For these reasons this is a popular professional defense.

The biggest disadvantage of this defense is that a team must have the strength to overcome pressure and counterattack from its own end. The team must be confident and organized because the ball is often within scoring range. A team that cannot clear the ball well or is weak in the air may regret using this defense. Another disadvantage is that the opponent often can maintain possession for extended periods of time. This has psychological effects and of course can be a factor when a team is behind. For these reasons, less skilled defenses avoid the retreating defense.

This defense is a logical choice against a team that is superior. The crowded conditions created near goal are difficult to penetrate by dribbling or short passing. The defense can be used to neutralize superior speed and quick counterattacks — if the defense organizes quickly.

Figure 167 Non-Retreating Defense

One variable in defensive tactics is the point of first organized resistance. Most players are not aware that this is even something that can be changed. They assume that the defense begins in the attacking end, with every inch of territory fought for. This high-pressure, fight-every-inch-of-the-way defense is a non-retreating defense, illustrated here. The less popular alternative involves a "tactical retreat". The defense offers first organized resistance beyond the midfield line and stiffens as the goal is approached. This defense has the advantage of not offering a large space behind the defense, giving the defense more time to organize, keeping the attack in front of the defense, and providing a more compact defense.

Factors Influencing Team Tactics

Opponent's Characteristics

Speed, Skill and Fitness

The speed, skill and fitness of an opponent are all important factors in defensive team tactics. Speed needs space. If the opponent is quicker they must be forced to play in a crowded area where their speed will not be a factor. If the defense retreats quickly, removes the space behind it, and forces the opponent to play through a packed area it can be successful. If the defensive team is quicker, it can play more aggressively. The speed will allow them to recover from mistakes and apply more pressure. However, quickness usually will not compensate for a lack of skill.

An opposing team with more skill must be forced to use those skills against greater numbers, in a smaller area and under greater pressure. The skill should be analyzed. Is it greater passing skill? What type of passes? Is it dribbling skill? What specifically makes their dribbling good? Is it deception, speed, ability to change direction? Is the opponent good at keeping possession and why? Are they good at combination plays? Under what circumstances? Do they use the whole field very well? With knowledge of an opponent, specific changes can be made to neutralize the advantage.

If the opponent is more physically fit, offensive and defensive tactics should be pursued that conserve energy. On offense this means playing a slower possession game and using more passing with less running and dribbling. On defense it means playing a more energy-conserving type defense; such as a packed defense around the penalty area.

Superstars

There are several approaches to an attacking team with one outstanding player (the "superstar"). The most common approach is to mark that person throughout the match. One player follows the star to keep them from getting the ball. This can be extremely frustrating for the marked player. Some teams seek to add to that frustration by using extremely physical defensive tactics. This may just be enough to cause the "superstar" to have a "bad day". Of course, the marking defender may not make much of an offensive contribution because of their defensive responsibility.

It is also useful to study the superstar's playing habits. Does the player strongly favor one foot for dribbling or shooting? Do they always try to go one way around a defender? Do they have a favorite move? Are they a reaction dribbler that thrives on avoiding aggressive tackles? With this information specific tactics can be used for defending. (See Chapter Five, Analyzing the Attacker.)

Know and point out the opposing team's better players. How do these players make things happen — by dribbling, by long accurate passes, or by shooting? By observing these things, common sense measures can be taken.

Passing

A team that relies heavily on short passing can be partially neutralized by deliberately bunching in the area of the ball. A highly organized system of tight markings around the ball also can be effective. A team that uses long passes must be countered by loose coverage away from the ball with an emphasis on covering the space, not the person. An alert sweeper can help run down through balls behind the defense.

Emotional Response

Emotion plays an important role in the motivation of a team. Motivation will affect all aspects of a team's performance. It is useful to know how an opposing team responds to being behind and being ahead. When behind, does the attacking team fall apart with members blaming each other, or do they get more determined and pull together? If they fall apart it is especially useful to score early. Some teams play much better when they are ahead — playing more creatively and with greater and greater emotion. It is obviously important not to fall behind when playing these teams, so that their confidence doesn't increase.

The Opponent's Offensive Team Tactics

How an opponent "plays position" is very important. A team that uses rigid positions with little movement is easy to mark. The contest breaks down into a series of one-on-one duels. If the defenders are better in these duels then the chances of a favorable outcome are good. If the opponent uses a less-structured offensive system, the defensive organizational task becomes greater. Open players may result not only from players beaten one-on-one, but also from confusion and lapses in concentration or ball watching. Organization, and in particular, communication become extremely important to the defense. A useful way to practice these skills is with keep-away games using forced individual markings.

One aspect of the offensive team of concern to the defense is their preferred method of getting the ball into the scoring area. Although today many teams penetrate by dribbling, short passing or combination play, the traditional approach is to play air balls into the penalty area from the flanks for another player to shoot or head into goal. This method depends on having a dominant player on the flanks (or being able to work another player free on the flanks) to center the ball. The second part of the combination is to dominate in the air (be taller or better at jumping and heading) in front of goal. Shutting down the attack on the flank or dominating in the air suppresses the attack. This whole form of attack has been developed into an elaborate science with its own vocabulary and books devoted to its explanation and perfection. Although not as popular today, centering the ball from the flanks is still an important means of scoring.

However, in modern soccer there is more variation in where the ball is centered from, how it got to that position, who centers it and how the ball is played into the middle. The ball is more likely to be passed specifically to a player (not centered blindly) and is more commonly played near the ground.

If the other team plays possession soccer you need to analyze how good they are at that style. Are they good enough to overcome your pressure? If so, or if that pressure cannot be sustained, then perhaps patiently waiting near the goal is the best advice.

If the opponent is an opportunist, then the opportunities must be minimized and provisions must be made to prevent capitalizing on those opportunities. The team should play with a deep sweeper. On turnovers the team must get back quickly and someone must immediately pressure at the ball to delay the attack.

Environmental Factors

For a review of the effect of environmental factors on team tactics, refer again to Chapter Four. The field size, surface type and condition, sun, and wind are all considerations. The emotional environment in which the game occurs is also a strong consideration. Especially important in this regard is whether the team is playing at home or away.

Characteristics of the Defending Team

"Defend when you are weak and attack when you are strong."
Sun Tzu

Characteristics of the defending team strongly influence defensive team tactics. Factors include: the team's speed, fitness, defensive skill, organizational ability, emotional characteristics, and preferred offensive tactics.

Speed

Speed affects defensive coverage most. More specifically, speed affects the need to provide coverage and the method of providing coverage for the defender at the ball. Fast players, when beaten, can often recover and get back into good defensive position, so the need to back up the player at the ball is less. They also can beat attacking players to through balls. As a result, the defense can play without a sweeper or without a covering teammate, or else the extra defender can double-team or cover other areas of the field. In effect, faster players allow the defense to be less concerned about support and covering space behind the defense.

When the team is slower than the opponent, the implications for defense are just the opposite. The team must have a well-organized system to cover for beaten defenders. Often this means playing an extra safety near the area of the ball behind the defense (the sweeper). Lack of speed always means more attention to defense — particularly support and organization.

Fitness

Fitness has many implications for the defense. With time, unfit players become slower than their opponents (Table 32). Fewer players can move to support an attack or help the defense. The team may be playing at a numerical disadvantage on offense and defense. As players fatigue they are more likely to make desperate, but less strenuous, all-or-nothing attempts at the ball. If the player is unsuccessful, they are so far out of the play that they see no need to hustle to recover. Good defending requires more work. As players fatigue they also make mistakes in judgement and no longer talk or have the field vision necessary to organize properly. For these reasons fitness is a critical element of the game. The fact that teams score most in the last 15 minutes of a match reflects this.

Effects of Fatigue on Defense

Decreased movements

- Fewer defenders get back
- Defenders get back more slowly
- Markings not established
- Markings not maintained
- Defenders beaten at ball and away

Consequences:

- Inadequate defensive numbers
- Open attackers

Mental changes

- Decreased concentration
- More emotional
- More likely to be apathetic
- Mistakes in judgement

Consequences:

- Poor organization
- Ball watching (open players unmarked)
- Open attackers
- Less cooperation

Table 32

Skills

A defensive team that is less skilled, particularly in the one-on-one conflicts must compensate. Superior speed and fitness will help in some situations. Excluding these, a defensive situation requiring even more offensive skill must be created. The only practical way of doing this is to make the attackers beat greater numbers of defenders in crowded conditions — a compact defense.

Organizational Abilities

The ability to organize is a defensive skill. This skill includes the following components: communication, leadership, individual responsibility and vision. Communication is essential for organizing a defense. Players must share information and point out covering responsibilities. This requires good vision, with players watching the entire field and the space behind them — checking the entire field every five seconds. Players must accept the responsibility of covering the player with the ball. This is the starting point of defensive organization. It also is useful to have a strong, respected, team leader that points out assignments and commands the defense. Frequently, particularly close to goal, this is the goalkeeper. In other cases, it is the sweeper or the player with most experience. These components are necessary for a team to be skilled in defensive organization. A well-organized defense can compensate for deficiencies in skill, fitness and speed.

Preferred Attacking Method

A team's preferred method of attacking influences its defensive tactics. For example, a possession-type offense is patient and involves everyone in the attack. Unfortunately, as a result, too few players may be back when there is a turnover. In this way, the offense will dictate the conditions present when the team goes on defense. The defense also influences the opportunities available to the offense. For example, a retreating defense creates the opportunity for fastbreaks. Therefore, a team may want to consider their offensive preferences when deciding on defensive tactics.

Figure 168 Photo by Phil Stephens

Chapter 8

Introduction to Set Plays

Kick-Offs

At the kick-off the defending team is in good position, with the whole team between the ball and goal. The attacking team is in a uniquely poor position to attack, with no players in the attacking end. For this reason, most professional teams quickly back-pass after the ball is rolled forward at kick-off (the rules require that the ball must first be played forward at the kick-off). The purpose is to draw out and weaken the defending team and to allow attackers to infiltrate the defense. However, at youth levels when the ball is played back, the team may not be able to move it forward again. For this reason younger teams usually continue to play the ball forward on the kick-offs. The less sophisticated just boot it as far as they can downfield. At a slightly higher level a player cuts across the middle from the flanks and an attempt is made to pass to this player. At a still higher level, the same pass is attempted after a back-pass. Teams that are confident in their ability to maintain possession and penetrate the defense usually play several back and square passes before attempting to move forward.

Throw-Ins

A throw-in is used to put the ball in play when an opponent kicks the ball across a sideline (touchline). The throw-in is made with both hands holding the ball from the sides. The ball is taken straight back over the head and thrown with one continuous motion, without twisting. Both feet must be kept on the ground, on or behind the line. In general, the throw-in should be taken quickly. The longer the delay the more likely players are to be covered. There are several throw-in "plays". The simplest is to throw the ball to a nearby teammate that is running at an angle down line. The second most common play is to throw the ball to a nearby teammate that plays it back to the thrower. In youth soccer it is better to always play the ball forward.

Free Kicks

F ree kicks are awarded for certain violations of the rules. Depending on the nature of the violation, a direct or indirect kick is awarded. A goal can be scored directly from a direct free kick, but must first touch another player on an indirect kick.

Defending

There is no special defensive tactic for free kicks when the ball is far from goal and cannot be played directly into the goal area. The defending team moves quickly to get between the ball and the goal. When a kick is taken close enough to be played into the scoring area, the defense usually forms a wall to block the path to goal. The purpose of the wall at closer distances is to protect the near half of the goal (Fig. 168 & 169, pg. 160 & 162). The goalie covers the far half of the goal. The number of people in the wall depends on the distance of the kick from goal and the angle. Usually the goalkeeper positions the wall, yelling at them to move right or left. Some teams have a field player direct the positioning of the wall from in front of the wall or from the nearest goalpost.

Figure 169 Defensive Wall

The normal function of the defensive wall is to assist the goalie by covering the near half of the goal. In this case the two-defender wall is helping the goalie by preventing dangerous low passes across the front of the goal. A single defender is similarly positioned on corner kicks.

Attacking

Free kicks outside of scoring distance should be played as quickly as possible before the defense can organize. When the free kick is closer to goal, more sophisticated tactics are often developed. The options are to shoot directly at goal, play the ball over the defensive wall or pass around the wall. The coach should feel free to invent various plays. However, keep in mind that the simpler the play the more likely it is to succeed. The players can make the plays more sophisticated by adding fake runs over the ball.

Corner Kicks

When the defending team kicks the ball over the endline, the attacking team is allowed a free kick from the closest corner of the field — a "corner kick".

Attacking

On offense, the ball is kicked into the middle of the goal area where an attempt is made to score. Classically, the scoring attempt comes from a header. There are two basic types of balls served into the center from a corner kick. The inswinger curves in toward the goal in its flight. The outswinger curves away from the goal mouth. Whether the ball swings in or out depends on which foot takes the kick. A right-footed kick from a right corner produces an outswinger—the left foot an inswinger. The left foot from the left corner produces an outswinger and vice versa. Most goals come from in-swingers played to the near goal post. Four attackers are positioned across the goalmouth. The usual play is to center the ball to the closest attacker who flicks it across goal for a teammate to smash in. Obviously, this is not a play for the unskilled.

On a kick that will swing away from the goal, the attacking players are usually positioned outside the penalty area — usually concentrated toward the far side of the goal. Runs are made as the kick is taken. A player is usually stationed on the far side of the penalty box just in case the kick comes through or is weakly cleared. Other players remain outside the penalty area to collect weak defensive clearances. Some teams position a player in front of the keeper to impede their movement to clear the ball.

An alternate attacking method is to play the ball short instead of kicking it directly to the middle. This player can often advance the ball closer to goal before centering it. This technique also disrupts the defensive markings in front of the goal. Of course, better teams will have far more plays developed than those outlined here.

Defending

There are certain positions that are always assumed by defensive players. A player is positioned inside of each goalpost. In small- sided games, the far post player is often omitted. A player is also positioned just off the endline 10 yards from the corner to prevent low crosses and help defend against the short kick.

The goalie is positioned one-half the distance to the far post. On outswingers the goalie is slightly off the line. On inswingers the goalie is on the goal line. The defenders that are not assigned a fixed position generally mark an attacking player, standing between them and the goal, impeding their movement to the ball. Some teams use a type of zone with players positioned close to the goal line and moving to the ball. This allows the players to react to the ball rather than the attacking players.

Goalkicks

If the ball crosses the endline and was last touched by the attacking team, the defending team is awarded a goalkick. The kick is taken from the small goalbox and must leave the penalty area before it is considered in play. Goalkicks are either played long or short. It is very beneficial to have a powerful kicker take these kicks. If the team has no one capable of kicking the ball long, the opponents will move up and anticipate the short kick. As a result, a team gets mired down in front of its own goal. If the ball can be kicked long, this threat will create the option to play the ball short. On the higher levels the short kick is preferred because possession is assured. A coach can develop several short kick plays designed to free an open player. Often the ball is played back to the keeper for security and because of the keeper's ability to throw the ball accurately or punt it long.

Figure 170 Photo by Phil Stephens

Chapter 9

Goalkeeping Basics

The goalkeeper is a unique player—the only one permitted to use their hands (when in the penalty area). Their position in the goalmouth makes them obviously important to defense. The most secure place for the ball on the entire field is in the goalie's hands. Less obviously, this position gives them a field perspective that makes them important to offense as well. The abilities to distribute the ball accurately by throwing, or over long distances by punting, contribute to their offensive value.

Ground Shots

The keeper shuffles sideways (side-steps) to get directly in the ball's path.

Scoop Technique (Figure 171)

Feet: The feet should be close enough to prevent the ball from going between the legs.

Hands: The hands should be behind the ball with the palms up. The ball should run up the hands and be scooped securely to the chest.

Head: The head should be steady and the eyes focusing on the ball.

Figure 171 Ground Shots Scoop Technique

Figure 172 Ground Shots
Kneeling

Kneeling Technique (Figure 172)

Feet: The body should be turned sideways, facing perpendicular to the path of the ball. Kneel, turning the upper body to face the ball. One knee rests on the ground in the path of the ball and even with the heel of the other leg.

Hands: The hands are together, palms facing upward. The ball rolls up the hands and the ball is scooped securely to the chest.

Head: The head should be steady with the eyes concentrating on the ball.

Waist-level Shots

Feet: The feet are shoulder-width apart with the weight evenly distributed. The knees are slightly bent with the weight forward.

Hands: The hands are together with the palms up. The arms curl around the ball and clutch it to the chest.

Head: The head is level and steady with the eyes focusing on the ball.

Figure 173 "W"
Catching Technique

The normal hand position for catching balls chest-high or above.

Head-high Shots

Feet: The feet are shoulder-width apart, with the weight evenly distributed, the knees slightly bent, the weight forward on the soles.

Hands: The hands are behind the ball with the thumbs together forming a "W" (Figure 173). The fingers are spread and relaxed. Relaxed fingers help grip the ball. Once the ball is caught it is brought to the chest.

Head: The head should be steady and the eyes watching the ball.

Deflections

Any ball that cannot be securely caught should be deflected. The ball is pushed to the side (Figure 174) or over the top (Figure 175) of the goal. When deflecting shots over the top of the goal, the ball is pushed upward with the palm. To get maximum height the body turns sideways to the incoming ball and the arm closest to the ball will lift it over.

Figure 174 Deflections

Figure 175 Deflections

Figure 176 Diving

See text.

Diving

The body weight shifts to the leg closest to the ball. This leg will push off. One hand positions behind the ball to stop it; the other is slightly to the side to hold it firmly. The ball is wedged between the hands and ground. The ball and arms land first helping to cushion the body's impact (Figure 177). To help secure the ball the legs are drawn up into the body and the ball pulled to the chest immediately after landing. Note: Young (10 and under) goalkeepers don't need to learn to dive.

Figure 177 Diving

See text.

Goalie Position with the Ball in Different Areas of the Field

When the ball is in the attacking third (greater than 70 yards distant) the goalie's basic position is 12 to 18 yards from the goalmouth. The goalie can act as a second sweeper for long through balls. In the middle third (40 to 70 yards) the goalie is 6 to 12 yards off the goal line. In the defensive third the goalie is 3 to 6 yards from goal. If the ball is on the flank 30 to 40 yards from goal the goalie should be positioned in the back half of the goal. This prevents crossed balls from floating over the goalie's head into goal. If an attack breaks clear from the defense on the flanks and advances toward goal the goalie must move to the near half — preparing to cut down the angle.

When to Advance Toward the Ball

Remember, a properly positioned goalkeeper seldom has to make spectacular saves. The goalkeeper should advance toward the ball to take

Figure 178 Cutting Down the Angle
A significant part of goalkeeping is simply being a movable barrier. The closer this barrier is to the ball the more goal is obstructed. The risk in coming out and cutting down the angle is being beaten by dribbling, by passing or by a shot made while advancing. The goalie's advance should be sudden, made only when there is no chance of another defender intervening, and when facing a single breakaway attacker. Once a decision has been made to come out, the distance should be closed as rapidly as possible. If during the approach, the attacker gives any indication of shooting preparation, the goalie should stop and assume a ready stance.

possession or narrow the angle (Figures 178, 179) when an attacker has cleared the last defender and is advancing to goal. The goalkeeper advances on a line between the ball and the center of the goal when the threat is in the middle of the field. When the threat has developed from one of the flanks the angle of advance is such that the near half of the goal is protected. The goalkeeper should stop advancing and achieve a balanced position when the attacker is preparing to shoot. The goalkeeper should stand up, becoming as big as possible. Be patient and wait for the attacker to move first.

Figure 179 Cutting Down the Angle

Breakaway!

The only time the goalie is on their line is during a penalty kick. By being off the line and patrolling the box the goalkeeper decreases the space behind the defense. By being closer to the defense the goalie is able to come out and clear balls with kicks, sliding tackles or headers. The goalkeeper can turn many potential breakaways into desperate looking through balls. The keeper should not attempt to do too much with these loose balls, as there is considerable risk if the opponents regain immediate possession. The opposing forwards often dictate when a goalie should come out.

The goalie watches for the forward on a breakaway to push the ball too far, especially when the forward is just breaking clear of the defense. The goalie can spring forward and clear the ball.

When the forward puts their head down this means either there is a shot coming or the player has lost control of the ball. If the forward is in control and is therefore judged to be shooting, the keeper should assume a ready position to respond to the shot (Figure 179, pg. 170). If the player has lost control, the goalie should quickly move forward to close the distance and if possible get possession of the ball.

When a forward is clear of the defense, the speed of the goalie's approach is approximately equal to that of the attacker. It is particularly important to approach a forward, who is moving slowly and with control, in a cautious manner. The angle of approach should be at an angle from the center. This approach will help keep the attacker from cutting to the middle. When a forward is not quite in control but the goalie cannot get to the ball first, a slide into the player's feet can result in possession or block the shot. In the slide, the body should be on its side — making as large a barrier as possible. The feet always are used to discourage movement to the middle, with the hands protecting the near post. The eyes should be kept open and should not be obstructed by the outstretched arms. When moving quickly start the slide two or three yards before the point of impact and slide through to the impact. This lessens the chance of injury.

Handling Crosses

The goalkeeper's position will depend on where the cross is originating. The closer the ball is to goal, the closer the goalie is to the near post.

Figure 180 Handling Crosses, Punch

On corner kicks the goalie is about half-way between the posts, about 3 yards off the goal line. The goalie must wait until the ball is kicked before moving. The goalie moves late and quickly, attempting to take the ball at its highest point (Figure 181). A one-footed take-off allows the keeper to jump higher. The goalie should punch the ball clear when uncertain about balance or footing and when the area is too crowded to securely catch the ball. If in doubt, punch (Figure 180) the ball! In punching, the bottom half of the ball should be struck, sending it high and far. With a one-fisted punch, the goalie has greater reach but cannot get as much power as when using both fists.

When in doubt, punch! If you are uncertain about your ability to hold on to the ball for whatever reason (crowd, wet ball), punch it. A single-fisted punch will allow the goalie greater reach but the ball may be cleared shorter or mis-hit. A two-fisted punch will give more certain contact, greater distance and greater accuracy. Punch the ball high and wide. Strike the ball just beneath its center.

Figure 181 Handling Crosses

Distribution

When the goalkeeper gets the ball the team is, by definition, on offense. The goalkeeper should quickly assess the field situation before distributing the ball. Often

On crosses or corner kicks the goalie is normally positioned in the back-third of the goal for a better view of play and because it is easier to move toward the ball than back up. Get a running start and catch the ball at its highest point. Move through the point of reception and raise the leg for protection. Bring the ball immediately to the chest.

Figure 182 Distribution, Bowling

Like any good pass, a pass from the keeper should be accurate, well-timed and easy to control. Punts give the best distance but lack accuracy and are difficult to control. The sling-throw has reasonable distance and is accurate but the passes may be difficult to control. The bowling technique shown here is only good for short distances but is accurate and easy to control.

Figure 183 Distribution

The greatest advantage the goalie has is the ability to use their hands. The safest place for the ball on the field is in the goalie's hands. The hands and arms also allow the keeper to distribute the ball accurately. The most common throw is a side-arm slinging motion. The motion is like throwing the discus, but without a body spin.

the best choice is to quickly throw (Figure 183) the ball to an open player on the opposite side of the field. Blindly punting the ball for distance is to be discouraged unless the opponents are pulled up, presenting an offensive opportunity or preventing any short passes. If there are no passing opportunities, the goalie should wait for the attackers to spread out. When distributing the ball, the goalie should make it as easy to control as possible — roll the ball "bowling-style" when possible (Figure 182).

Playing the Ball to the Keeper

The first choice of any defender intercepting or stealing the ball in the defensive third should be to pass to the keeper (Figure 131 & 132, pg. 117). When the goalkeeper has the ball it is as safe and secure as it will ever be. The goalkeeper has a unique position from which to see the entire field and the offensive opportunities. The goalkeeper can pass accurately with the hands or drive the ball deep with long punts (Figure 184).

Communication

The goalie's unique position behind the defense gives them a better view of the developing attack. There are times when they should communicate what they see to the appropriate defenders. In particular, they should communicate the presence of unmarked players on the side away from the ball or unnoticed behind the defenders. The goalkeeper can often communicate when and who should quickly cover a threat in front of goal. The goalkeeper should communicate their intentions when moving to catch or clear the ball or when they want to be passed the ball. The goalkeeper can encourage the team to move forward quickly when a ball is cleared.

Figure 184 Punting

The punt is the goalie's longest, but least accurate pass. A two step approach is all that is needed. The power comes from the leg swing and the forward and upward movement of the body (The goalie is airborne during follow-through for long kicks). Hold the ball out straight, drop it without spin from the left hand. Let the ball drop low before striking it with the laces of the kicking foot. The ball should leave the foot when it (the foot) has risen to a 45 degree angle.

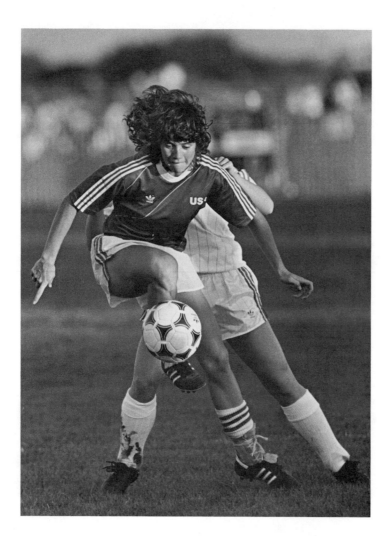

Figure 185 Photo by Phil Stephens

Chapter 10

Basic Soccer Skills

Trapping (Receiving)

General Principles

- Get in line of flight
- Adjust position back and forth to select surface (if possible)
- Cushion ball (like catching raw eggs)
- Land ball 2-3 feet away, ready for next action (ready position)

Selecting a trapping surface

Three categories of balls:

- Level balls
- Descending balls
- Rising balls

Level 1 (ground-to-knee-height balls)

Level balls:

Use the inside of the foot below the ankle bone, (the same surface used for passing) to stop the ball, then withdraw the foot, absorbing the force off of the ball or redirecting it as necessary.

Mistakes:

- Missing ball entirely (not concentrating on the ball)
- Using wedge trap for ground balls (doesn't allow repositioning of ball)
- Ball bouncing too far (touch only comes with practice)

Descending and rising balls:

- Smother the ball at the moment it strikes the ground
- Position the toe up, forming a wedge
- Pre-position the foot in the path of the ball's flight
- The ball can also be caught and cushioned with the instep (a difficult skill, illustrated in figure 185, pg. 174.

Mistakes:

- Not positioning the foot in the path of the ball and as a result missing the ball entirely
- Positioning the foot too high and having the ball bounce under it

Level 2 (thigh-height balls)

Level and descending balls (Fig. 186):

- Use the middle portion of the thigh
- Withdraw the thigh as the ball strikes it
- Ball may bounce slightly up and forward, landing in a ready position

Mistakes:

- Ball often does not strike center of thigh and bounces off to either side instead of staying in front of player.
- The ball is often not cushioned well and bounces too far away from the player. This skill only comes with practice.

Figure 186 Thigh Trap

Receiving the ball on the thigh is a fairly difficult skill to perform under pressure. The receiving surface is not that large and it is curved, so any balls that hit off-center go astray. All parts of the thigh between the knee and hip are used, depending on the ball's height and angle of flight. The thigh is positioned perpendicular to the angle of the ball's flight. The thigh is quickly withdrawn a short distance at the moment of impact. It is difficult to use the thigh to accurately redirect the ball away from a pressuring defender.

Level and rising balls:

Turn the leg out 90 degrees and use the soft fleshy surface to absorb the shock of the ball. The ball does not usually bounce away.

Level 3 (Chest-height balls):

Level ball:

Using the middle of the chest, expand the chest and draw the shoulders forward before the ball strikes. Exhale and collapse the chest at impact to cushion and catch the ball.

Descending ball (Fig. 187):

Catch the ball on upper chest, leaning and rocking back slightly with the impact to cushion the ball. Attempt to make the ball bounce straight up and then land just in front of the feet.

Rising balls:

Bend forward and deflect the ball down with the lower chest or the abdomen.

Mistakes:

- Ball strikes off center and bounces left or right. Correct this by concentrating on the flight of the ball and practicing.
- Ball strikes too high, hurting the throat. This is due to not positioning the body properly in the flight of the ball.
- Ball bounces too far away, due to not cushioning properly.
- Chest gets sore. Try practicing with a slightly de-

Figure 187 Chest Trap

As with most traps, the body surface that is receiving the ball is positioned perpendicular to the ball's angle of approach. The receiver generally tries to move so the ball can be received on the top half of the sternum. The ball is cushioned by collapsing the chest (exhaling) and swaying the upper torso backwards. By twisting the trunk as the ball is received, the ball can be redirected away from an opponent or even passed a short distance.

flated ball (or volleyball).

Heading

Principles:

- Defensive striking surface is high on the head to aim high and long.
- Offensive heading uses the flat of the forehead to aim ball level or down.
- Cock the body at the waist (like the hammer on a pistol) for power— use a short powerful stroke.
- Keep the mouth closed, eyes open.

Offensive heading: (Fig. 188)

- Get in the flight of the ball
- Keep the eye on the ball.
- Cock the body at the waist.
- Accelerate through the ball.
- Punch the ball with the forehead.
- Head down to score, or level for passing.

Defensive heading: (Fig. 189)

Apply same principles, but hit the ball higher and aim

Figure 188 Offensive Heading

In the crowded scoring area it is difficult to get a good jump, concentrate on the ball and cock at the waist. The power may come from the body's forward movement, a twisting motion at the waist, and the neck snapping forward. With offensive heading more height is required in order to get the ball moving downward.

Figure 189 Defensive Heading

The power for this defensive, clearing header came from the defender's forward movement, a twisting motion at the waist, and from the neck. The ball is struck beneath its center from a point near the hairline.

high to get distance.

Jumping and heading: (Fig. 190)

- Jump early.
- Cock the body while jumping (like having your racquet back in tennis before the ball arrives).
- Concentrate on the ball.

Mistakes in heading:

- Letting the ball strike you, not you striking the ball.
- Closing the eyes.
- Opening the mouth.
- Not having the body cocked.

Figure 190 Jumping and Heading

To get the maximum power in heading the body is bent at the waist. The back arches and the knees bend, like a drawn bow.

Dribbling

The basic skills are straight line dribbling, changing speed, changing direction, and using fakes.

Basic Skills:

Straight line dribbling:

How close the ball is kept depends on the closeness of the opponents. The ball is carried forward at the end of the stride. The toe is pointed down, the carrying surface is the top of the foot near the bottom of the laces, and the feet are turned slightly in—pigeon-toed (Fig. 191 & 74, pg. 180 & 67). Adjustments for when the ball goes sideways are made with the inside of the foot using the ball of the big toe and the outside of the foot by the small toe.

Mistakes:

- Dribbling in a duck-like fashion, using only the inside of the feet.
- Tapping the ball forward. The ball should be gently carried forward with the foot.

Figure 191. Straight-line Dribbling

In straight-line dribbling the ball is usually carried ahead just a little as the foot is landing. The foot is turned slightly inward and the ball contacts the top outside surface of the shoe just above the four smaller toes. Carrying the ball in this fashion is very natural. The inside surfaces (commonly used by the beginner) are only used for minor corrections (when the ball strays sideways) and to make sharp changes of direction. Admire the head-up posture.

Figure 192 Cutting

Being able to change direction quickly and sharply is an essential soccer skill. The most common method is to sharply hook or stab the ball to one side with the top inside of the foot as shown here. See also figure 206, 193.

Figure 193 Cutting

Changing direction with the outside of the foot is often done in conjunction with a fake in the opposite direction. In this photo the upper body says, "I am going to the right," while the lower body charges off to the left. The surface used is the outside top of the foot near the little toe.

Figure 194 Cutting

Another extremely useful method of changing direction is by playing the ball behind the supporting leg. This is very effective because the ball is entirely out of reach of the opponent — an unstoppable move. Also see figure 93 on page 82.

Changing speeds (stopping and starting):

Stopping is best accomplished with the sole of the foot. The body leans back and the sole of the foot is pressed on the top of the ball to stop it (Fig. 84, pg. 74). The ball is generally started again with the inside of the foot pushing the ball forward (Fig. 195, pg. 182).

Changing direction:

The ball is cut inside (Fig. 192) and outside (Fig. 193) with the inside and outside of the foot. The more sharply the ball must be cut, the farther back on the inside or outside foot surface the ball is played (Fig. 89, pg. 79). Also, as the ball is cut more sharply the foot is place farther ahead of the ball. This is practiced best by dribbling through cones using only one foot to control the ball.

Another important change of direction is putting the body in reverse. Reversing direction is best accomplished by stopping the ball with the sole of the foot and rolling it backwards as the body reverses (Fig. 84, pg. 74).

Fakes:

Three simple fakes are the pull-push, the stepover and the shooting fake.

Pull-push or stopping fake

This fake is used to simulate stopping or reversing direction. It is useful with a defender on your shoulder, when stopped or moving. The back half of the sole of the foot away from the defender is used to stop the ball and roll it backwards. After rolling the ball back the foot comes off the ball, stops its motion and then pushes it forward (Fig. 195).

Figure 195 Stopping Fake

Step-over fakes

These fakes are used to simulate passes or sudden changes of direction. One foot is passed quickly in front of the ball. This rapid movement should simulate a kick. The foot can either move clockwise or counter-clockwise around the ball (either moving toward or away from the supporting leg). When the motion is towards the other leg, the second part of the fake is to use the outside of the foot that passed around the ball to change direction (Fig. 197). When the initial kicking motion is away from the other leg, the inside of the opposite foot carries the ball forward ("scissors move", fig. 196). The ball must be kept close to the body—ideally it is beneath the body at the time of the stepover.

Shooting fake

The shooting fake is used to beat defenders and to temporarily get the defender out of one's path so a real shot or penetrating pass can be made. The

Figure 196 Stepover Fake #1

You can do the step-over fake in one of two ways — make a clockwise or counter-clockwise movement of the foot around the ball. Here the foot moves away from the body, then the ball is carried forward with the opposite foot. This is also known as a "scissors move".

Figure 197 Stepover Fake #2

Sweeping a foot quickly in front of the ball toward the other leg is a very simple and effective fake. The motion can be used to simulate shooting, passing, changing direction or sudden acceleration. If the defender responds, use the outside of the foot to move in the opposite direction. The sweeping motion is easier if the ball is under you, not in front of you, when you begin.

shooting fake is performed by pushing the ball slightly forward and away from the body. The player approaches the ball as if to kick it, cocks the leg and swings it forward stopping behind or beside the ball. If the defender moves to block this simulated shot the attacker can quickly cut the ball to the other side. The fake and the cut are often combined in one motion as shown in Fig. 198 & 199.

Inside of the Foot Pass

This is the most important pass in soccer because of its accuracy.

Figure 198 Shooting Fake

Because preventing goals is very important shooting fakes are very effective, especially near the goal. The motion is the same as an instep shot. Usually the attacker fakes a shot past one side of the defender, then cuts and goes to the other side.

Figure 199 Shooting Fake

There three positions—starting position, striking position, and follow-through.

The Three Basic Positions (procedure):

Starting position:

The ball is one step in front of the player. The foot that is to strike the ball is behind the player, on the ground (Fig. 200). The body's weight is behind the ball. As the kicking foot starts toward the ball the foot turns out 90 degrees and comes up about two inches off the ground.

Striking position:

The body faces the target. The ball is on a line between the body and target. The toe of the slightly bent supporting leg points at the target (Fig. 72, pg. 65).

The leg that will strike the ball is turned out 90 degrees, with the knee bent. The striking foot is about three inches off the ground, the foot turned out, the toe of the striking foot is pointed slightly up (Fig. 73, pg. 66). The body's weight is slightly behind the ball. The ball is struck in the middle with the back half of the foot. Figure 201 shows the ball just leaving the foot.

Follow-through:

After the ball is struck the lower leg continues forward but starts to rotate. The foot will continue forward and up. It will rotate from pointing straight to the side to pointing straight forward, at the target. The upper leg rotates from pointing straight to the side to pointing straight forward. As the leg rotates it will gradually come up and will bend more at the knee (Fig. 202). The weight is now forward on the planted foot. The follow-through is extremely important for accuracy and power.

Mistakes:

- Not turning the foot out 90 degrees when the ball is hit.
- Hitting the ball too far forward on the foot, or more with the instep. As a result the ball will not go straight. The ball will also not be hit solidly.
- Foot too low as it strikes the ball—the ball comes up.
- Player leans back instead of following through. The ball may come up in the air, the pass lacks power, and the accuracy is less. Usually caused by not rotating or bending kicking leg.

Figure 200 Inside-of-the-Foot Pass

The beginning of inside-of-the-foot pass is similar to a golf putt. Your foot (the club) sweeps forward in a straight line toward the target. This, together with the flatness of the striking surface, are the basis for the pass's accuracy.

Figure 201 Inside-of-the-Foot Pass

The back half of the foot or heel strike the ball just below its center. At the moment of impact the foot is raised slightly, turned out 90 degrees, toe raised slightly, and the kicking leg is bent. The foot continues straight forward for a short distance, until the ball leaves. As the leg continues forward the kicking leg naturally begins to turn because it is attached at the hip. It is just beginning to turn in this photo. (Continued...)

- Legs are not slightly bent and do not bend with the follow-through. A straight kicking leg will ruin the follow-through.
- Body and ball are not lined up facing the target. Ball hit awkwardly to the right or left of target.

Figure 202 Inside-of-the-Foot Pass

In the follow-through the kicking foot continues forward and up. Let the knee bend. If you keep it straight you will lean back. Leaning back causes the ball to go up and decreases the power. Power comes from the leg and movement of the body's center of gravity forward as the kick is made. In the final position the toe of the kicking foot points at the target. The non-kicking foot is always pointing at the target.

Shooting with instep (long passing)

The technique for long passing and shooting are the same.

Major Points:

- Kicking surface is the hard bony arch where the shoe laces are tied.
- For a low shot (the best) the striking foot must be at or above the ball's center.
- The approach is at an angle, depending largely on the size of the shoe. The upper body may have to lean away from the ball if the foot is long. This is necessary to have the bony arch strike the center of the ball, yet avoid having the toe catch in the grass.
- Power comes from a combination of the leg extension and the body moving forward as the ball is struck, transferring the body's momentum to the ball. A long running approach and a large backswing are not necessary.
- The planted foot should be beside the ball, pointing at the target. To kick the ball up, place this foot behind the ball and strike below the ball's center .
- Keep the head down (watching the ball) and steady.
- Follow through. After striking the ball the body should continue forward landing on the kicking foot with the toe pointing at the target.

Mistakes:

- Not watching the ball.
- Leaning back as the ball is struck (ball goes up). The best shots are low.
- Not following through. This may result from leaning back. There is loss of power and accuracy.
- Making a big running approach.
- Kicking with the toe not the bony arch.

Figure 203 Instep Kick

The instep kick is used for long kicks and shots demanding power. The motion is more natural for the hip than the inside-of-the-foot pass. The kicking surface is the bony arch of the foot beneath the shoe laces. Most of the power from the kick comes not from the extension of the kicking leg, but from forward movement of the entire body as the kick is made. With the most powerful kicks the body flies forward (Fig. 204, pg. 188). To get this power doesn't demand a long run, but rather a coordinated movement of the kicking leg as the body accelerates through the ball.

Figure 204. Follow-through

The follow-through with instep shots will vary, however, with the hardest shots the kicker continues forward after the shot. This creates a maximum momentum transfer. The player lands on the kicking foot.

Rules

There are only 17 official soccer rules. These are abridged.

Law I. The Field of Play

The soccer field is rectangular, not more than 130 yards in length (minimum 100 yards) and not more than 100 yards in width (minimum 50 yards). At each end are a goal area containing a goal, a penalty area, a penalty spot, and six yard box used for taking goal kicks. There is a semicircular arc at the edge of each penalty box behind which players must stand when a penalty kick is taken (see law XIV). In the center of the field is a 10 yard center circle contain-ing a center spot. The game is started from this spot at the beginning of each half and after goals. The opposing team must be out of the circle until the ball is put in play (rolls one circumference, see law VIII). There is a line that divides the field equally in two. Teams must be in their own half at the start of the halves and when play is restarted after goals. There are also small arcs in the corners of the fields into which the ball must be placed on corner kicks (see law XVII).

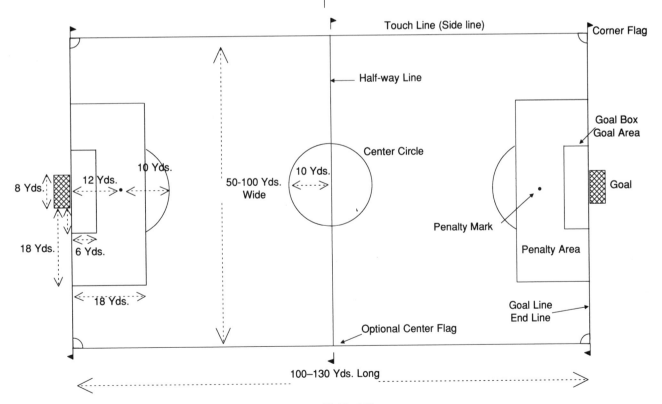

Fig. 205. Field of Play

189

Law II. The Ball

The ball is made of leather or synthetic material. Its circumference is between 27 and 28 inches and its weight between 14 and 16 ounces for a full sized ball.

Law III. Number of Players

A team is composed of 10 players and a goalkeeper. Any player can play goalkeeper if the referee is notified. The goalkeeper must have a distinguishing jersey. In international play only two substitutions are allowed. Once substituted a player cannot return (international play only). Substitutions rules are determined by local leagues (and vary greatly). In most leagues substitutions are unlimited. Players must come in at the midfield line and only on goalkicks, when a team has a throw-in, after goals, and after an injury. There must be 7 players to have a legal match.

Law IV. Player's Equipment

A player should not wear anything that might injure themselves or another player. For this reason, referees inspect players and have them remove watches and jewelry. The goalkeeper must wear distinguishing colors. Studs must be rounded, at least 1/2 inch in diameter and not longer than 3/4 inch. Shin pads will soon be required equipment.

Law V. Referees

The referee is completely in charge of the game. He/She keeps the time and the official scoring. The referee is responsible for administering penalties for rule infractions or misconduct. The referee need not stop the game for an infraction if he/she feels it would give an advantage to the offending team (the notorious "play on"). The referee may halt the game for injury or call it off because of bad weather, spectator interference or misconduct. All decisions are final.

Law VI. Linesmen

There are two linesmen. Their chief responsibility is to indicate when the ball is out of play, which side gets the ball, and whether it should be put back in play by a throw-in, corner kick, or goal kick. They also look for offsides violations and any rule infractions missed by the referee. Only the referee can stop the game and the referee decides if there has been a rule violation. The linesmen communicate information with their flags. (For some lower level games parents or spectators act as "club"linesmen.

Law VII. The Duration of Play

An adult game consists of two 45 minute halves. (Some ignorant officials are suggesting an 80 minute game for women. Youth games are shorter. Some high schools play 20 minute quarters.)

Law VIII. The Start of Play

A toss of the coin determines which team chooses between having the ball first (kicking off) or defending one end of the field or another. After a team scores the other team restarts play with another kick-off from center. The teams switch ends at half-time. The ball must roll one circumference to be in play. The kicker can't retouch the ball until it has been touched by another player (redo kick-off if a violation). A goal cannot be scored directly from a kick-off. The game is restarted after some stoppages (non-rule violations) by a drop-ball (similar to a face-off in hockey).

Law IX. Ball In and Out of Play

The ball is only out of play when it has entirely crossed one of the field boundaries. It is still in play if it bounces off a goalpost or an official. Play is also stopped when the referee blows their whistle.

Law X. Method of Scoring

The team that scores the most goals wins. If equal, or no goals are scored the contest is a draw. A goal is scored when the entire ball crosses the line between the goalpost. On a goal, the ball may not be propelled into the goal by a hand or arm of the attacking team (except the goalkeeper from his own area).

Law XI. Offside

A player is considered offside if he is nearer his opponent's goal than the ball at the moment the ball is played, unless: 1) They are in their own half of the field 2) Two opponents are nearer their goal line (including the goalkeeper) 3) The ball last touched or was played by an opponent 4) The ball was received directly from a goal kick, corner kick, throw-in or drop ball. A player is not called offside unless, in the opinion of the referee, he/she is gaining an advantage by being offside or is interfering with play or an opponent. The penalty for being offside is an indirect free kick.

Law XII. Fouls and Misconduct

The following offenses are penalized by a direct free kick from the point of the foul (see next law for explanation of direct free kick):

- Kicking or attempting to kick an opponent

- Tripping an opponent

- Jumping at an opponent

- Charging into an opponent in a dangerous manner

- Charging into an opponent from behind (unless being obstructed)

- Striking or attempting to strike an opponent

- Holding or pushing

- Contacting the ball with hands or arms (except keeper)

Should any of the above offenses be committed by the defensive team in the penalty area a penalty kick is awarded.

An indirect free kick is awarded for the following offenses:

- Playing in a dangerous manner

- Bumping (charging) an opponent when the ball is not in playing distance and there is no attempt at playing it

- Obstructing (preventing them from getting to a ball that you can't reach either) an opponent

- Attacking, tackling or charging the goalkeeper unless he is not in control of the ball, is obstructing an opponent, or is outside the penalty area

- Delaying by the goalkeeper (four step limit)

A caution is issued a player if: (An indirect kick is awarded for the last two infractions and is optional on the first)

- Enters or re-enters the field without the referee's permission

- Shows dissent (by word or action) with a referee's decision

- Unsportsmanlike conduct A player can be sent off the field for:

- Serious foul play or violent behavior

- Use of foul or abusive language

- Persistent misconduct after being cautioned If the game is stopped to send off a player, it is resumed by an indirect free kick by the opposing team.

Law XIII. Free Kick

There are two types of free kicks — indirect and direct. The difference is that on indirect kicks a team cannot score directly from the kick — the ball must first be touched by another player (same team or opponent's team). The referee signals an indirect kick (as opposed to a direct kick) by a raised arm. On free kicks the opposing team must be at least 10 yards away unless standing on their own goal line. For a team taking a free kick from their own penalty area the opponents must be outside the penalty area and at least 10 yards distant. The ball is in play after it has rolled one circumference and cannot be touched again by the kicking player until touched by another player.

Law XIV. Penalty Kick

A penalty kick is awarded the attacking team when the defending commits any foul that would result in a direct free kick in their penalty area. The free kick is taken from the penalty spot. No player other than the defending keeper may be in the penalty area or within 10 yards of the ball (the arc at the top of the penalty area is 10 yards from the penalty spot). The goalkeeper must remain stationary on his line until the kick is taken. The person taking the kick cannot play the ball a second time until it has been touched by another player. The ball must roll one circumference before it is live. If the ball rebounds off the goalkeeper or goalpost into the field of play it is live. For any violation of this law:

- If by the kicker, an indirect free kick is awarded the defending team.

- If by the attacking team other than the kicker and a goal results, the kick shall be retaken.

- If by the defending team and a goal doesn't result, the kick shall be retaken. Time shall be extended to allow a penalty kick to be taken.

Law XV. Throw-In

When the ball crosses a sideline (touchline) the opposing team puts the ball back into play with a throw-in at the point where the ball went out of bounds. The player must keep both feet on the ground, on or behind the touchline. The ball must be thrown in one motion, using both hands, delivering the ball over the head. A goal cannot be scored directly from a throw-in. The player making the throw cannot play the ball again until it has been touched by another. Opponents can not attempt to distract or impede the thrower. If the throw is bad the other team is given a throw-in at the same spot.

Law XVI. Goal Kick

When the attacking team kicks the ball out across the defense's end-line a goal kick is awarded to the defending team. The kick is taken from the right or left side of the goal box depending on which side of the goal the ball passed. Opponents must be outside the penalty area on the kick. The ball is not in play until it has passed outside the penalty area. The kicker can not play the ball again until it has touched someone else.

Law XVII. Corner Kick

When the defending team is responsible for the ball passing across their own end-line a corner kick is awarded the opposing team. The kick is taken from the corner of the field closest to where the ball went out of play. The ball must be in the small quarter circle marked at the corners. Opposing players must be back at least 10 yards at the time of the kick. The ball is in play when it has rolled one circumference. The kicker can not play the ball again until it has touched another player. Goals can be scored directly from corner kicks.

Figure 206 Photo by Phil Stephens

Glossary

Advantage rule: When a referee allows play to continue, instead of awarding a free kick after a foul is committed, because in his judgement it is to the attacking team's advantage.

Attacking third: The offensive end of the field; the end of the field containing the goal that a team is attacking.

Back (pass, position): Towards the goal a team is defending.

Bait: To lure, to tempt, to provoke an opponent (usually into making an attempt at the ball).

Ball watching: Literally, to stare at the ball while ignoring everything else that is going on. A common bad habit.

Beat (defender): To go around an opponent. To move past them, and get between them and the goal they are defending.

Beatable defender: A defender that is vulnerable to being beaten, as a result of their defensive technique.

Blind side: The area not seen by a player because of the direction they are facing.

Boots: British term for soccer footwear.

Breakaway: To burst through the last line of defense and approach the goal, temporarily unopposed.

Centering pass: A pass (usually in the air) that is made into the area immediately in front of goal.

Challenge: To make an attempt to get possession of the ball.

Charging: Use of the shoulder to bump an opponent in an attempt to get the ball — theoretically legal.

Combination plays: Coordinated pass-move combinations executed by two or more players. The most common example is the wall pass.

Cone defender: A defender that remains motionless (like a traffic cone) as an opponent approaches with the ball.

Corner kick: See Law XVII. A free kick awarded the attacking team when the defending team is responsible for the ball going out of bounds across the line at their end of the field. The ball is put back into play from the closest corner of the field with a free kick.

Create space: An action that results in opponents leaving a certain area of the field. That area, now without any opponents, is the created space. Space is commonly created by moving when covered. The defender follows, creating a space.

Cross: A ball directly passed (usually in the air) from an area on the side of the field into the goal area.

Crossfield (runs, movements): Any movement that goes across the field, as opposed to a movement that goes along the field's long axis. Crossfield movements are important because they are difficult to stop, confuse the defense, and create useful space.

Cut: To sharply move the ball sideways with the foot. This is usually done with a quick chopping movement.

Dead space: An area without space — defenders present.

Glossary

Defensive shell: A defense that is organized very close to the goal it is defending and is only reluctantly drawn from that area.

Defensive third: The area (third) of the field closest to the goal being defended.

Depth: Using the field's length. An attack with depth uses combinations of through and back passes to stretch out the opposing defense.

Destroy possession: To knock the ball away from an opponent. This temporarily upsets the progression of the attack (gaining time for the defense), even though the team may not gain possession of the ball.

Double-team: Two defenders working together to get possession of the ball.

Dribble: In U.S.A. — to carry the ball with the feet, including the activity of trying to go around an opponent. In Britain— to attempt to beat an opponent while carrying the ball with the feet.

Endline: The end-of-field boundary lines.

Fake: An imitation of a soccer action. A fake is usually an abbreviation of a normal soccer motion, such as shooting.

Far post: The side of the goal farthest from the ball.

Fastbreak: A quick counterattack.

Feint: See fake.

Flanks: The areas toward the sides of the field.

Flat: To be in a line straight across the field.

Formation: A fixed, orderly arrangement of the field players. Usually players are placed in three parallel lines — forwards, midfielders and defenders. The number of players in each line, listing the number of defenders first, is the formation's name. A "4-3-3" has four defenders, three midfielders and three forwards.

Freekick: After many rule infractions the opposing team is allowed to put the ball back into play with a kick from the site of the infraction. The opponents must be 10 yards away at the time the kick is taken. See Law XIII.

Full-court pressure: A type of defense in which the defending team organizes and pressures around the opponent's goal and along the entire length of the field in hopes of creating a turnover.

Full-field pressure: Same as full-court pressure

Funnelling: A defensive tactic in which the defending team continues to get closer together as they approach the goal being defended.

Give-and-go: To pass the ball, sprint, then receive a return pass. (See Wall pass.)

Goalmouth: The opening in the front of the goal.

Goal-side position: On defense, to be in a position between the ball and the goal being defended.

Guiding: When defending at the ball, to take a position that will prevent or discourage the attacker's ability to move in a certain direction. A position is usually taken that prevents movement to the middle and encourages movement away from goal.

Halfbacks: Formations use three parallel rows of players. The middle row of players are the halfbacks or midfielders.

Heads-up: Literally, to play with head up when in possession of the ball. A player with their head up can see the field and the activities of other players and make much wiser decisions about what to do.

Heading: To propel the ball with the head. The usual passing surface is the forehead.

Inside-of-the-foot pass: A passing technique that uses the inner surface of the back half of the foot to accurately push the ball to a teammate. (Also called Push-pass.)

Jockeying: Same as guiding (above).

Juggling: A ball control exercise in which different body surfaces (feet, thighs, head) are used to keep the ball continuously in the air.

Keeper: The goalkeeper. A soccer player with special privileges (can use his/her hands to control the ball in the penalty area) who is the guardian of the goalmouth.

Kick-off: How play is started at the beginning of each half and how the game is restarted after a goal has been scored. The kick is taken from the center of the field. See Law VIII.

Making an angle: An action when you have the ball. You move the ball very quickly to either side to temporarily get clear of a defender to pass the ball forward. When free of the obstructing defender you can pass to more of the field (bigger angle).

Making up ground: Movement of a defender toward a pass recipient while the ball is in flight.

Man-on-man markings: A defensive system in which each defender is responsible for covering and continually following a single attacking player.

Mark: Pertains to defenders. To cover, to guard. A defender marks by assuming a position between the attacker and the goal being defended.

Midfielders (halfback):   See halfbacks.

Near post: The side of the goal closest to the ball.

Neutral (situation, position):   A one-on-one in which both the attacker and defender are separated by space and are either stopped or moving in the same direction at the same speed. This is a situation in which neither the attacker or defender has a significant advantage.

Numerical advantage: To have more players than the opponent in an area.

Nutmeg: To push the ball between the legs of an opponent.

Off the ball: The players that aren't in the area around the ball.

Offside trap: A defensive play. The defenders move forward trapping attackers in offsides positions. The defending team is awarded a free kick for this rule infraction.

Offsides: See Law XI.

On-side: In a position that is not offsides — generally, an attacker is on-side if they are behind the ball (between the ball and the goal they are defending).

One-on-one: The attacking player with the ball and a single opposing defender.

One-touch passing: To pass the ball with a single stroke (touch) — without stopping it first.

Open: To have space. To be in an area free of opponents.

Overlap: A particular run (movement) made by an attacking player that does not have the ball. The attacking player runs forward from a position behind the ball.

Own goal: To score on one's own goal — to accidently put the ball into the goal being defended.

Pace: The speed given to a ball when it is passed.

Passing lane: With respect to the player with the ball, those parts of the field to which a pass can be directly and easily made. The passing lanes are avenues traced from the ball past defenders in the ball's immediate vicinity.

Penetrate: To advance the ball toward the opponent's goal.

Play at an angle: This term usually refers to the position of a defender close to the defender at the ball. To be positioned behind and to one side of the defender at the ball.

Playing off (an attacker):   A term that refers to the action of the defender at the ball. To not mark tightly, to be a comfortable distance from the attacker—usually about six feet.

Post: The vertical bars comprising the sides of the goalmouth.

Pressure: An action of a defender. To be close to an attacker. The term also implies more aggressive behavior.

Push pass: A pass made by pushing the ball with the back-half of the inside surface of the foot.

Reaction distance: The distance a player can move before an opponent can react.

Read (a defender):   To evaluate. A player with the ball "reads" the defender's responses to their actions.

Recover: The action of a defender or the defending team. To move to a position between the ball and the goal being defended.

Retreating defense: A defense that falls back, sets up, and selectively defends the area immediately in front of goal.

Run: A movement made by an attacking player. A "run", as opposed to lesser movements, is usually sudden, dramatic, or long.

Screen: To use the body to shield or protect the ball. The term is also used to describe a situation where a goalie's view of the ball is blocked — "You're screening me!"

Set play: A planned series of offensive movements or actions executed at a free kick.

Shielding: To use the body to protect the ball.

Sideline: The side boundary line of the soccer field.

Sideways-on: A defensive stance in which the defender faces the same direction as the attacker and takes a position near the attacker's shoulder.

Slide tackle: A technique used by an individual defender to get the ball. The defender slides to the ground and uses the feet or legs to block and hold the ball.

Square: A position relative to the ball, approximately perpendicular to a line drawn between the ball and goal. In easier terms, to either side of the player with the ball.

Stance: The body position of an attacker or defender.

Support: To help. On offense, teammates "help" the player with the ball by creating safe passing options. On defense, teammates "help" by taking a position to back-up the defender at the ball.

Sweeper: A special defensive player that acts as a roving safety behind the other defenders.

Switch (fields):   To move the ball to a new area — usually the other side of the soccer field.

Tackle: A defender's technique. To attempt to get possession of the ball by using the feet.

Takeover: A combination play in which two attackers move towards and past each other and the ball is moved from one player to the other.

Through pass: A pass that goes in the general direction of the goal being attacked.

Throw-in: A method of putting the ball back into play after it has passed over one of the sidelines. The ball is thrown into play using both hands, drawing the ball straight back over the head. See Law XV .

Total football: A style of playing soccer in which players have no positions or formations. The only way to play that really makes any sense.

Touchline: The side boundary line of the soccer field.

Turnover: To lose possession of the ball.

Two-touch: An attacking technique in which a player uses one touch to control the ball and a second contact to pass the ball .

Vital space: The (unmarked) area from which most goals are scored. The area is slightly larger than the penalty area.

Wall (free kicks): A line of defenders that is positioned ten yards from the ball on free kicks within scoring distance. The purpose of the wall is to help block up part of the goalmouth so the goalkeeper's task is easier.

Wall pass: An offensive combination play in which a player passes to a teammate, sprints around a defender, then receives the ball back. (Also known as a give-and-go.)

Width and depth: A tactical term that refers to use of the width and length of the field on offense. In a classic offensive build-up, the attacking team should have players spread out over the entire width and much of the length of the field and the ball should be moved freely across the width and length of the field in order to draw out the defense.

Wing: A label for an attacking player (forward) that attacks along the sides of the field.

Zone (defense): A team defensive system in which defenders are responsible for covering an area (as opposed to marking and following a single attacking player).

Index

A

B

C

T

Acknowledgements

This book was produced on personal computers with word processing software (Microsoft Word®), page layout software (Xerox Ventura Publisher®), and with drawings created in Micrografix Designer®. The drawings were created by my wife, Carolyn Emory. She also designed the covers, helped edit the text and provided psychological and logistic support. Photographs were contributed by Kingsley LaBrosse, Phil Stephens and myself. All Minnesota Kicks photos were contributed by Kingsley, most National Team photos by Phil. Alan Merrick reviewed the contents of the book and made helpful suggestions. Michael Poquette, and John Sexton Sr. from Sexton Printing, provided technical assistance. My current soccer team, Krona S.C., served as guinea pigs for most of the ideas in this book. Some of the team members are featured in the photographs — Alex Iden & Deb Parsons (one-on-one situations), Mindy Mayerchak (goalie), and Tracy Savage (skills).

Mark Catlin & Carolyn Emory

Afterward

This book and the ideas in it are a product of an obsessive personality. Every instructor I have ever had in soccer was more than willing to tell me what to do, but none could tell me why. I found that profoundly disturbing. Many questions were accumulating and festering in my subconscious by the time I attended a USSF license course in 1976. That course didn't provide the answers, but it did give me an undefined term — "space" — that was the magic catalyst. During my first year of medical school everything started coming together and a theory was born — all soccer tactics are based on decisions relating to space. I started producing handouts containing my ideas for my team, the University of Minnesota Women's Soccer Club. The handouts were subsequently organized into a booklet and bound. In the following years, they were revised and produced in several different formats. With the help of a friend (Kingsley LaBrosse), photographs were added in 1979. The sixth rendition of the text, *Understanding Soccer*, was produced in small numbers in 1984. With each printing my ideas have been refined and additional material added. The Sun Tzu quotations popped up after I played a computer game called, "The Art of War". Quotations from the book (by the same name) featured in the game, immediately struck me as being relevant to soccer. For this version additional photographs have been provided by Phil Stephens whom I met while taking pictures at the USA Cup in Blaine, Minnesota.

I am grateful to everyone that has purchased this book in its various renditions and has helped to spread the word. Thanks for the many positive comments you have made — they have helped me to feel less of a soccer heretic. Unfortunately, I can't resist a few last heretical statements: If you understand the game of soccer you will realize the importance of movement and realize how restrictive and unnatural our current system of positions and formations is. Instead of imitating others, and perpetuating this outdated system, we in the USA should aspire to play "Total Football", a unique and superior style. My teams do it, yours can too.

The Art of Soccer Order Form:

Item	Price	#Desired	Total Cost
Soft cover	$15.95		
Hard cover	$29.95		
	Grand	Total	

Postage, Handling & Tax are included in the price.

Make Checks Payable To:

"Soccer Book"

Mail Check & Order Form To:

**Soccer Books
PO Box 4756 – 01
St. Paul, MN. 55104**

Please Mail My Books To:

_____

Name

_____

Address

_____

_____

City State Zip

7478